4² SQUARED ALUMNI

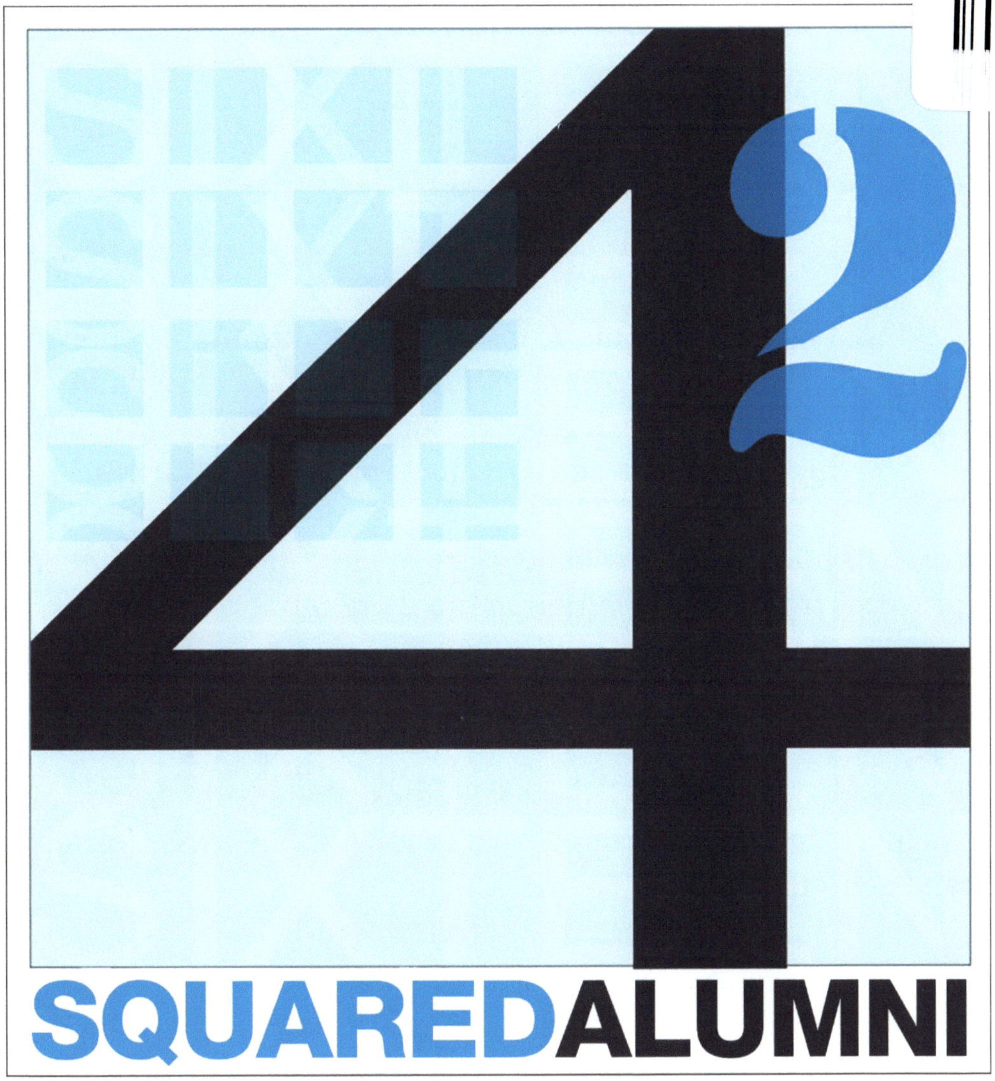

August 28 - September 28, 2019

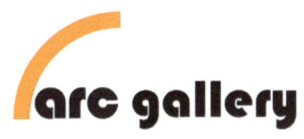

Curator's Statement

SquaredAlumni 2019 brings together eight of the most popular alumni from previous *Four-Squared* exhibitions at Arc. Each artist will be exhibiting four works. The exhibition is a reflection of the Arc partners' strong and abiding interest in supporting San Francisco Bay Area art, artists and community. During fundraisers and special events, all of the artists in the exhibition will be
donating about 20% of their proceeds to any beneficiary organizations. Arc will be donating 100% of the gallery proceeds from this exhibition to those organizations.

Curator:

Michael Yochum is the co-founder of Arc Gallery & Studios, along with partners, Priscilla Otani and Stephen Wagner. He is the managing partner for Arc Fine Arts Consulting, connecting local businesses and collectors with SF Bay Area artists.

Catalog designed by Michael Yochum
Logo image by Mitchell Confer
© Arc Gallery 2019

Featured Artists

Elizabeth Ashcroft

Jeffrey Galinson

Katja Leibenath

Paul Morin

Linda Raynsford

Eric Rewitzer

Rebecca Szeto

Melissa Wagner

ARTISTS RECEPTION
Saturday, September 7th, 7-9pm

TEEN VAN FUNDRAISER
Friday, September 13th, 3-5pm

GROUPMUSE
Sunday, September 15th, 6:30-9pm

ARTIST DISCUSSION & CLOSING RECEPTION
Saturday, September 28th, 12-3pm

Squared Alumni
August 28 - September 28, 2019

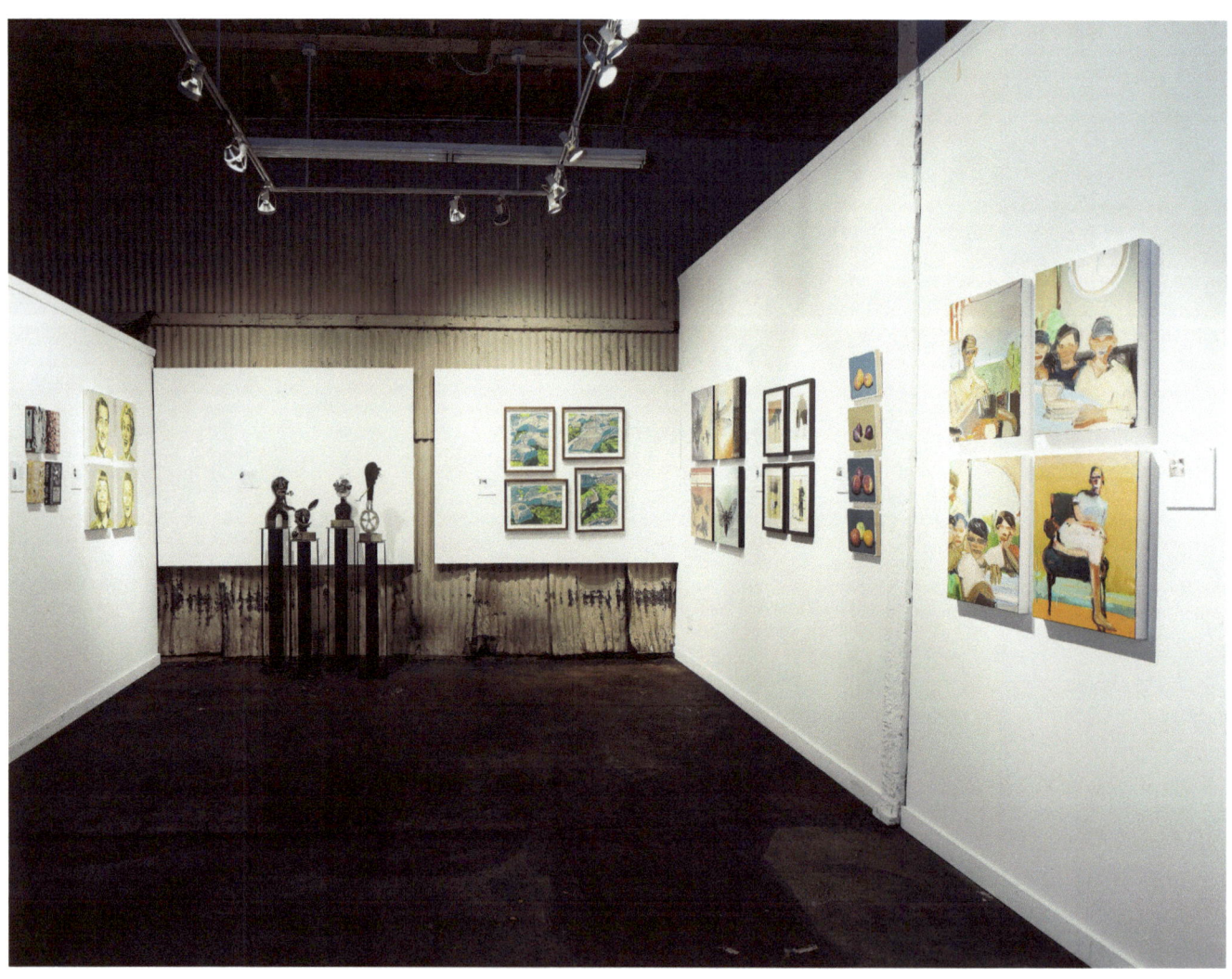

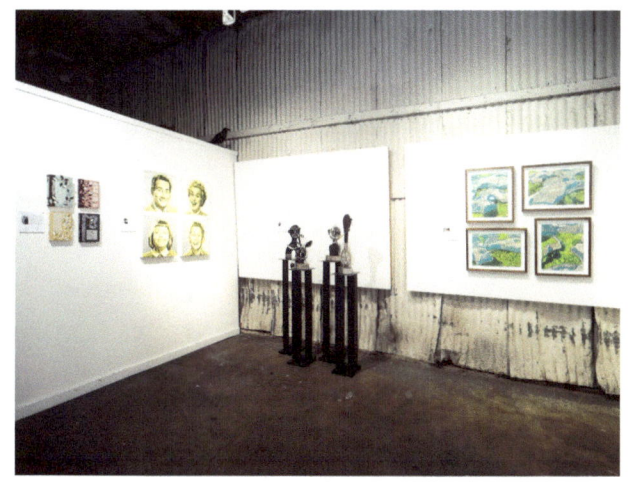
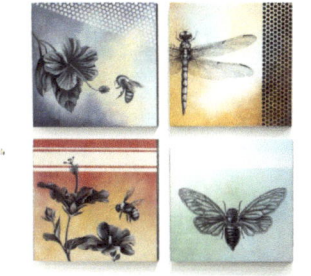
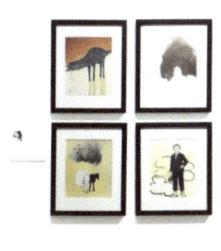
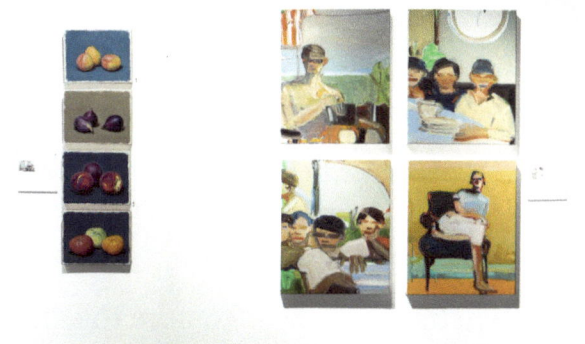
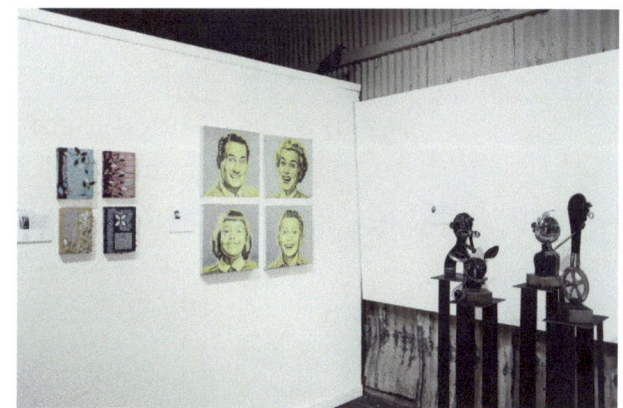
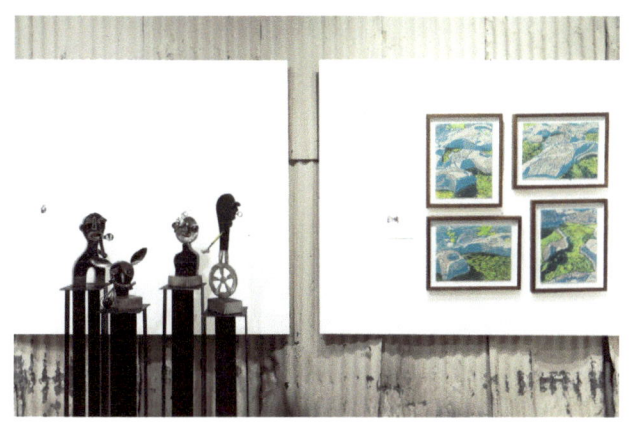
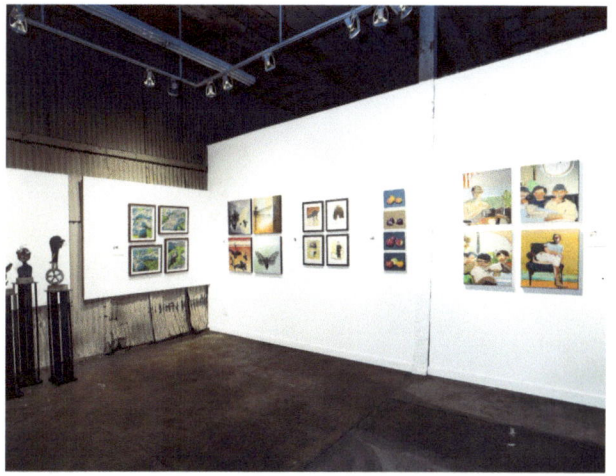

Elizabeth Ashcroft

Words Are Like Leaves Are Like Ideas

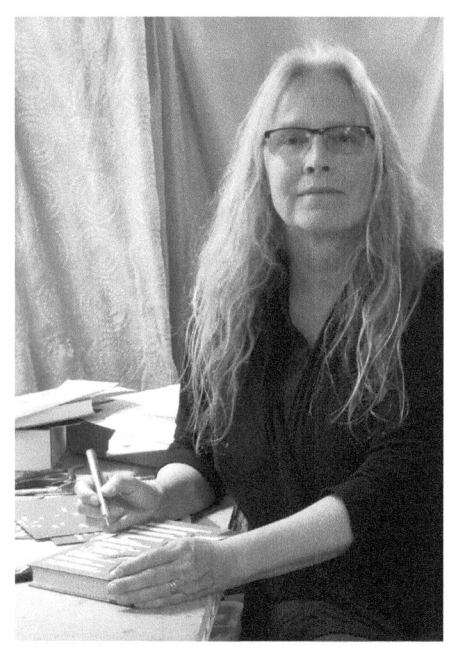

As part of my ongoing *Note To Self* series, these works incorporate mirror shards alongside a grouping of word/phrase fragments, a kind of found poetry if you will. The words are culled from the book itself, cut out, and pasted into new contextual relationships. My aim is to form opportunities for unexpected thought/word connections while offering glimpses of a refracted/reflective view of oneself and ones surroundings.

I often incorporate leaf shapes into my altered books – I like the shape, book pages are called leaves, and trees are the source of paper. I'm also attracted to the leaf's symbolic roles, as part of the tree of knowledge for example, along with its complex natural role including transforming light into energy.

In relation to my personal artistic process, I aspire to achieve a balance that hovers along the edge where intention and serendipity meet. Where I can conceive of a creative path ahead while remaining open to an evolving destination – a path not dissimilar to that of a leaf as it falls from the tree.

website: http://www.artbyashcroft.com/
email: eastudio@comcast.net

photo credit for images of art: Dennis Hearne

EDUCATION

1983   BFA, Printmaking, Massachusetts College of Art, Boston, MA

SELECTED EXHIBITIONS

2019
- *Bound & Unbound 5: Altered Book Show,* University of South Dakota, Vermillion SD
- *10th Annual Book Exhibition*, Marin MOCA, Novato CA
- *Alphabet Soup*, Studio Gallery, San Francisco CA
- Artspan Juried Auction, SOMArts Cultural Center, San Francisco CA

2018
- *Yosemite Renaissance 33*, Yosemite National Park Museum, Yosemite CA
- *Art & The Written Word*, Studio Gallery, San Francisco CA
- *Book As Art: Pulp*, Periodicals Gallery of the Decatur Library, Decatur GA
- *Secrets, Lies, & Disinformation*, Arc Project Gallery, 1246 Folsom, San Francisco CA

2017
- *SquaredAlumni*, Arc Gallery, San Francisco CA
- *City Scape & 94109*, Studio Gallery, San Francisco CA
- *Boundaries & Balance*, ACCI Gallery, Berkeley CA
- *Snap*, Arc Gallery, San Francisco CA
- *Night Light*, Studio Gallery, San Francisco CA

2016
- *Delicious*, Studio Gallery, San Francisco CA
- *Plus One*, Studio Gallery, San Francisco CA
- *Look! Book Art*, The Healdsburg Center for the Arts, Healdsburg CA
- *Solidarity-Unity-Acceptance*, 111 Minna Gallery, San Francisco CA
- *Curated State*, Exhibition & Real Estate Staging, San Francisco CA

2015
- *FourSquared 2015*, Arc Gallery, San Francisco CA
- *Bound & Unbound III*: Altered Book Show, University of South Dakota, Vermillion SD
- *Yosemite Renaissance 31*, Yosemite Museum Gallery, Yosemite CA
- *Absence and Presence*, SF Center for the Book, San Francisco CA
- *6th Annual Altered Book Show*, Marin MOCA, Novato CA
- *Impulse*, Arc Gallery, San Francisco CA
- *City Scape & 94109*, Studio Gallery, San Francisco CA
- *36th Annual Mini Works on Paper Show*, Jacksonville State University, Jacksonville AL
- *Seeing Red*, Village Theater Art Gallery, Danville CA

2014
- *AIn Other Words*, Pop-Up Gallery @ Autobody Fine Arts, Alameda CA
- *Impulse*, Arc Gallery, San Francisco CA
- *Red*, Russian River Art Gallery, Guerneville CA

COLLECTIONS

- Shakespeare Collection, University of Denver Library, Denver CO
- McCabe Library, Swarthmore College Library, Swarthmore PA
- Smithsonian Institution Libraries. Washington DC
- City of Decatur Book Art Collection, Decatur GA

AWARDS

2018   Yosemite Renaissance 33, Second Place
2012   College of Arts and Sciences Award, 34th Annual Mini Works on Paper Show, Jacksonville FL
2010   Certificate of Honor, Community Artist & Visionary, SF Board of Supervisors

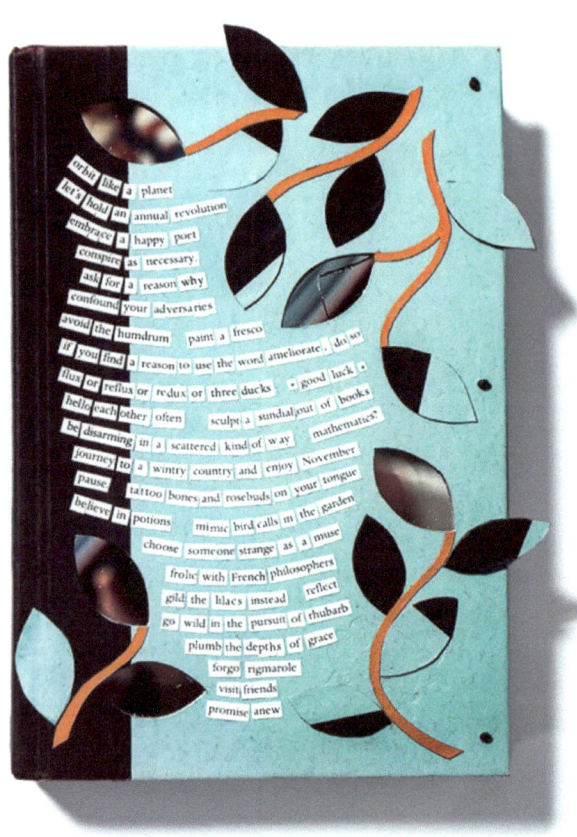

Ameliorate
altered book
approximately 9" x 6"
$550

Words Are Like Leaves
altered book
approximately 8.5" x 5.5"
$550

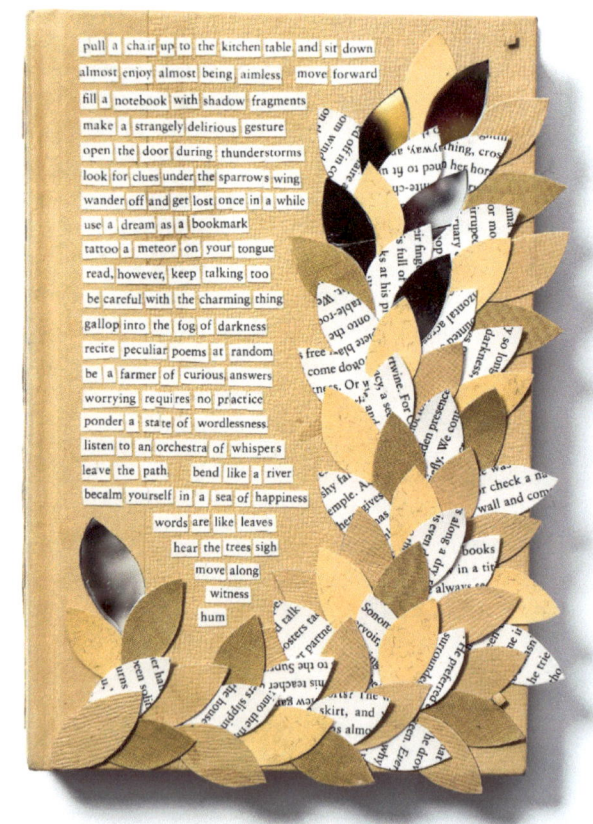

Elizabeth Ashcroft

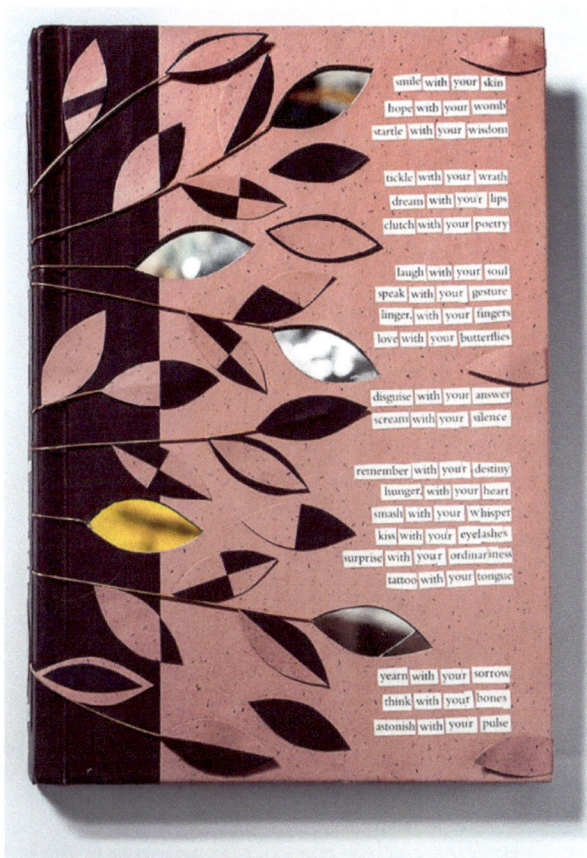

Look With Your Words
altered book
approximately 9" x 6"
$550

The Grace Option
altered book
approximately 9" x 6"
$550

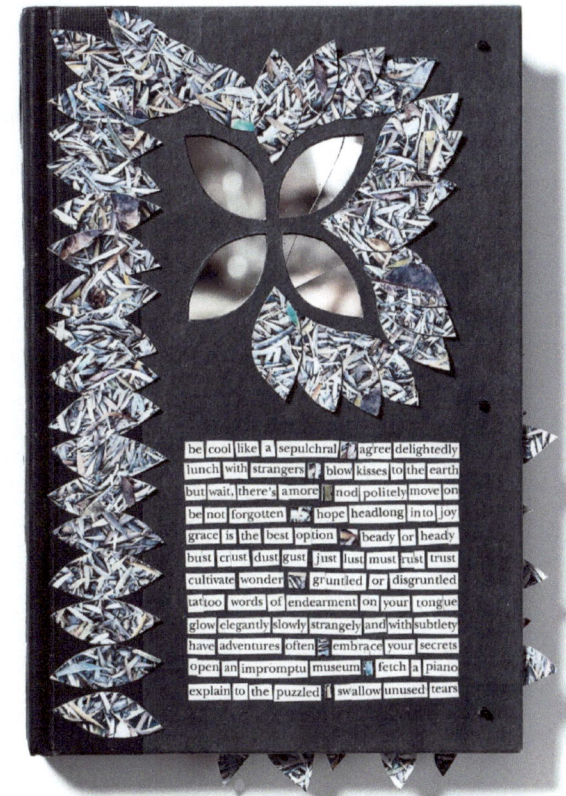

Elizabeth Ashcroft

Jeffrey Galinson

Trios

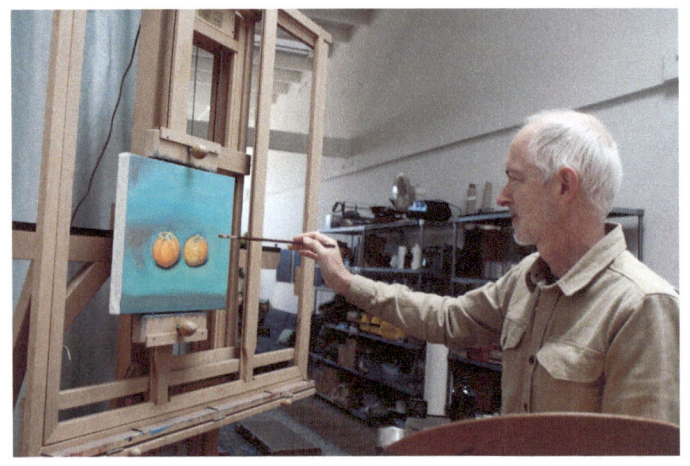

Painting directly from life presents the artist with a unique challenge: to attempt to convey the feelings that are evoked by the motif as it is considered by the eye, distilled by the mind, and given over to the hands to set down again in physical form as a two dimensional image; one that retains a fidelity to what is seen but is also uniquely transformed.

The fruits and vegetables chosen for this series present an additional challenge: to capture the colors, textures and fullness of volume while they are at their maximum capacity and dynamism. The degradation of color and form occurs quickly, especially in those objects where the interior has been exposed. Given this constraint, as well as the quick drying properties of working on paper, it was necessary that each of these paintings be executed in a single day.

I chose to depict the objects in groupings of three, as I have always felt that this arrangement creates a pleasing dynamic and harmony. All four compositions are massed similarly, with the object on the right somewhat apart from the two on left.

website: http://www.jeffreygalinson.com/
email: jeffrey.galinson@gmail.com

EDUCATION

1990	MFA, Graduate School of Figurative Art, New York Academy of Art, New York NY
1987	BA, University of Colorado, Boulder CO (Philosophy); Phi Beta Kappa)

JURIED EXHIBITIONS

2000　*Artists Guild 2000 All California*, juried exhibition, San Diego Museum of Art, San Diego CA
　　　　juried by Charles Reid. One of 69 works selected from a pool of 1200 submissions

GROUP EXHIBITIONS

2018	*FourSquared*, Arc Gallery, San Francisco CA
	Alphabet Soup, Studio Gallery, San Francisco CA
2016	*Delicious*, Studio Gallery, San Francisco CA
2012	*Take Home A Nude*, New York Academy of Art, New YorkNY
2000	*Food in the Library,* Athenaeum Music and Arts Library, La Jolla CA
1996	*Special Arrangements, Pat Brauer and Jeffrey Galinson*, The Promenade Gallery at the Bushnell, Hartford CT

OPEN STUDIOS

2003-19 San Francisco Open Studios, ArtSpan, San Francisco CA

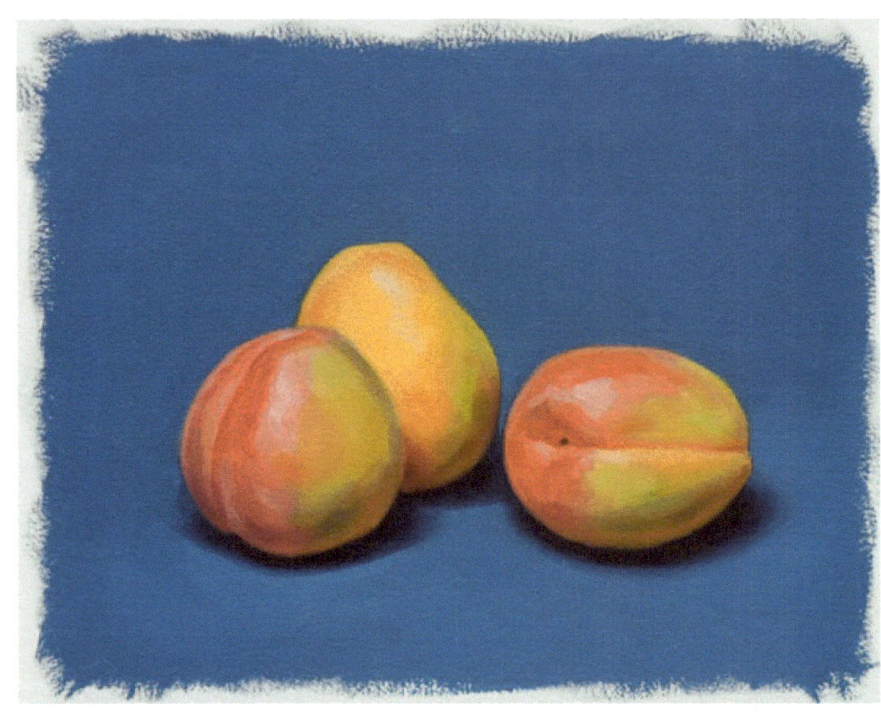

Apricots
oil on paper mounted on panel
8" x 10"
$550

Figs
oil on paper mounted on panel
8" x 10"
$550

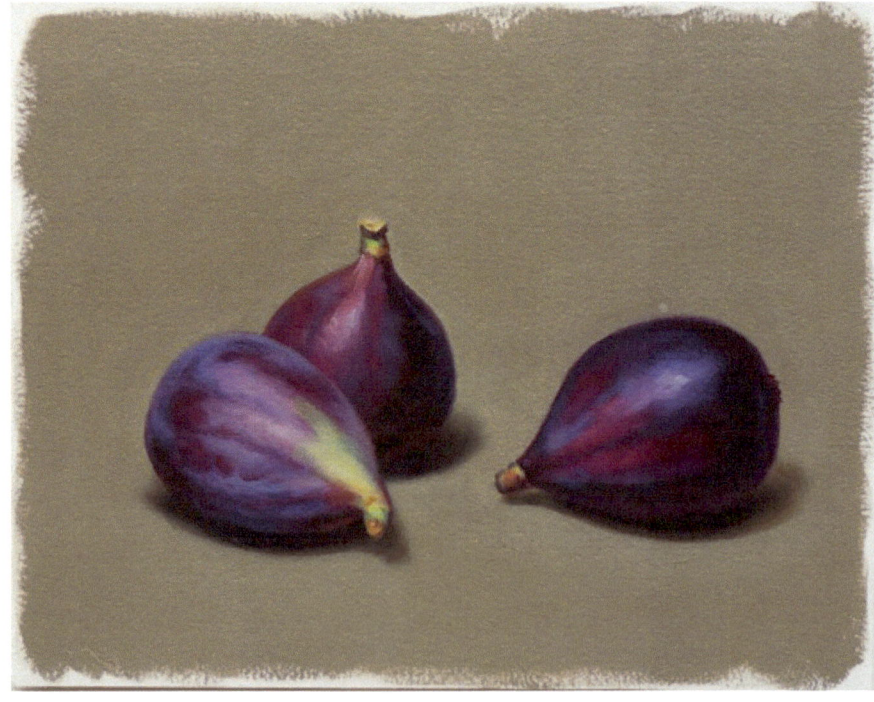

Jeffrey Galinson

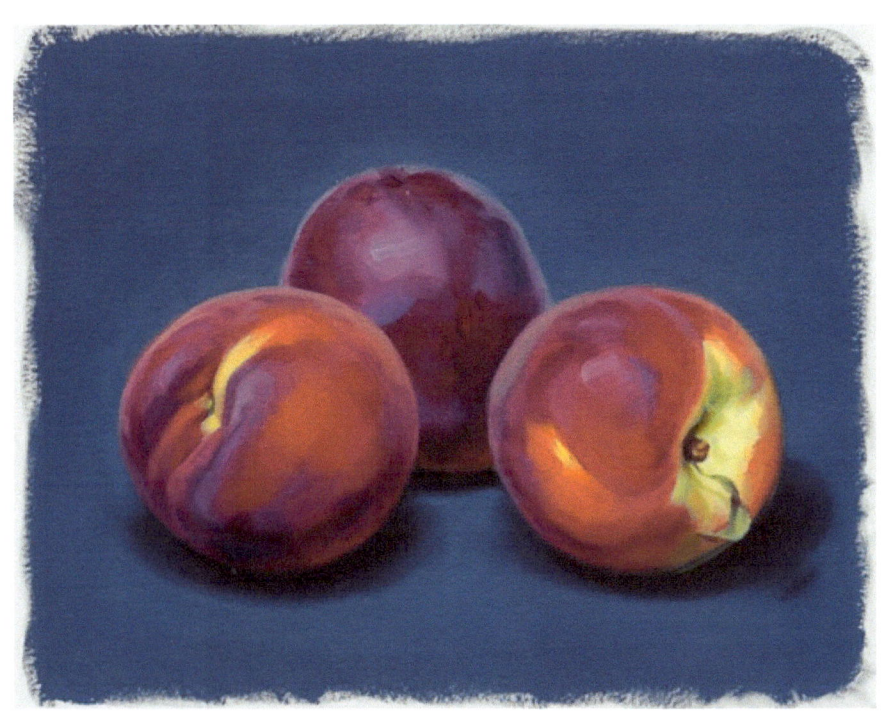

Peaches
oil on paper mounted on panel
8" x 10"
$550

Tomatoes
oil on paper mounted on panel
8" x 10"
$550

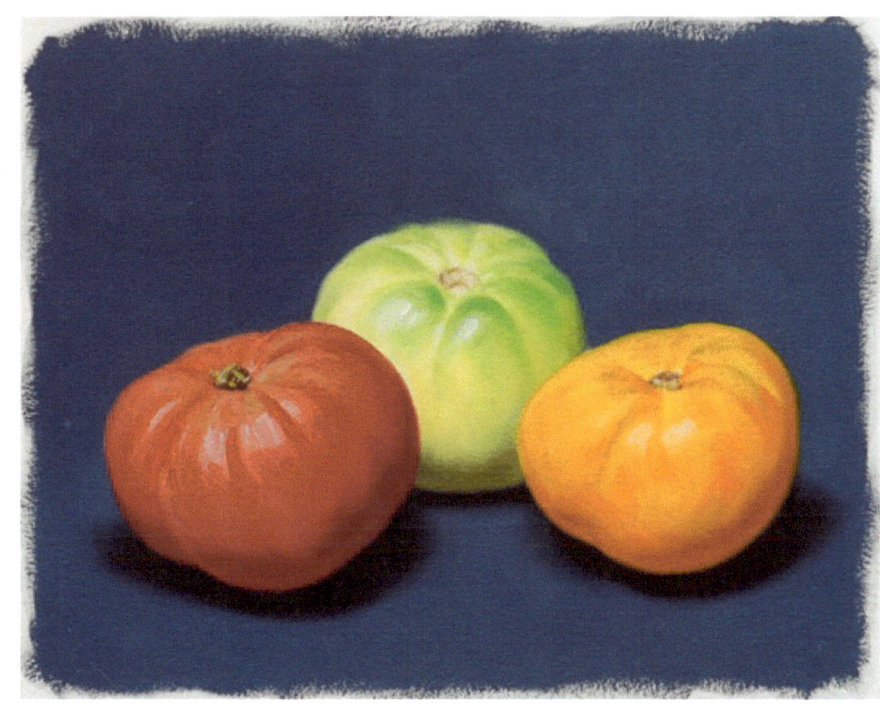

Jeffrey Galinson

Katja Leibenath

Seated Figures

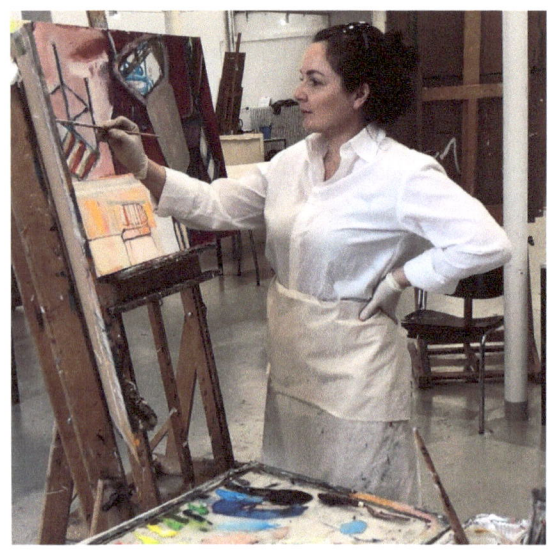

My paintings are figurative abstractions of either the human form or a specific place. I work from my own source material- photographs, sketches and plein air renderings of things I see on my travels. I translate this material into oil paintings over the course of many months in my studio. During the painting process the original object becomes obscured and less important, allowing something new and separate to emerge. The final painting is a record of my relationship to the process of painting itself, and marks the moment where subject becomes object and is ready for connection with the viewer.

Originally from Germany with a background in architecture and art, I have been painting in San Francisco since 2006. My work is part of public and private collections internationally and has been exhibited in New York, Los Angeles, Miami, and Atlanta, in addition to San Francisco.

website: http://www.katjaleibenath.com
email: katja@katjaleibenath.com

EDUCATION

1995 - 2000	Peter Behrens School of Architecture [fh-duesseldorf,de], Düsseldorf, Germany
	Dipl-Ing FH Innenarchitektur/ BA Interior Architecture & Furniture Design
1994 – 2015	European Academy of Fine Art [eka-trier,de], Trier, Germany/ Luxembourg (Drawing, Painting, Photography)

SELECTED EXHIBITIONS

2019
Kunstakademie Boehlen, Painting Residency with Joe Allen, Boehlen, Germany
Diamond Heights, Chinatown Alley Gallery, Sacramento CA (curated by Pamela Skinner)

2018
StartUp Art Fair SF, Hotel Del Sol, San Francisco CA
Introduction, Chinatown Alley Gallery, Sacramento CA (curated by Pamela Skinner)
Académie Européenne des Beaux Arts, Painting Residency with Joe Allen, Trier, Germany

2017
StartUp Art Fair SF, Hotel Del Sol, San Francisco CA
48 Pillars, Arc Gallery, San Francisco CA
Metropolis, Arc Gallery, San Francisco CA (curated by Matthew Frederick)
ArtSpan Selections, Heron Arts, San Francisco CA (SF Open Studios juried selction of 15 artists)

2016
SquaredAlumni, Arc Gallery, San Francisco CA
Salton Sea, Curated State, San Francisco CA
StartUp Art Fair SF, Hotel Del Sol, San Francisco CA

2015
Something Lost, Something Found, Curated State, San Francisco CA (two person exhibition)
Spotlight: Figure, Arc Gallery, San Francisco CA
The Way You Make Me Feel, a.Muse Gallery, San Francisco CA (curated by Lori Shantzis)

2014
Black and White Show, John McEvoy Fine Art, San Francisco CA
Soiree at Sunset, Sunset Magazine HQ, Menlo Park CA (benefit auction)
Large Figures, John McEvoy Fine Art, San Francisco CA

2013
Connect & Collect, San Jose Institute of Contemporary Art, San Jose CA (live auction)
Foursquared IV, Arc Gallery, San Francisco CA
Grimm at Dartmouth, Baker-Berry, Dartmouth College, Hanover NH
Katja Leibenath and Jessica Martin , Art Concepts, Walnut Creek CA (two person exhibition)

2012
Tiny, Studio Gallery, San Francisco CA
Sea Ranch Spindrift Gallery, Gualala CA
Introduction, JohnMcEvoy Gallery San Francisco CA (solo exhibition)
Grimm at Goethe, Goethe Institute, San Francisco CA

2011
Figure 8, Hang Gallery, San Francisco CA
San Francisco Fine Art Fair, Hang Art Gallery, San Francisco CA

2010
RED DOT, Miami Art Fair, Hang Art Gallery, Miami FL
Genius Loci, Hang Gallery, San Francisco CA (solo exhibition)
AF Contemporary Art Fair, Hang Art Gallery, New York NY

2009
Enormous Tiny Art, Nahcotta West Gallery, Los Angeles CA
Little Jewels, Huff Harrington Gallery, Atlanta GA

COLLECTIONS AND OTHER NOTABLE ACHIEVEMENTS

2019	The Passion Project – Podcast , Brightworks, San Francisco CA
2018	People and Places - The Paintings of Katja Leibenath - by Danielle Smith
2016	SF Open Studios Juror's Award (juror: Jill Manton, San Francisco Arts Commission)
2015	Zuckerberg General Hospital and Trauma Center, SFAC purchase - Permanent Collection, San Francisco CA
2010	Hereafter, Clint Eastwood movie 2010, art placement Hang Gallery, San Francisco CA

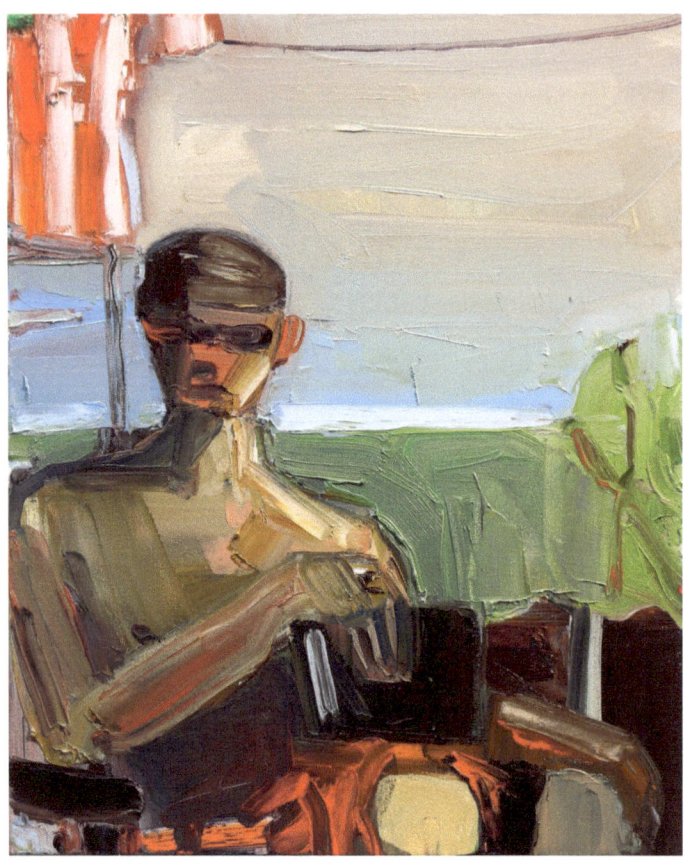

Seated Figure # 05

oil on canvas
20" x 16"
$1300

Seated Figures # 07

oil on canvas
20" x 16"
$1300

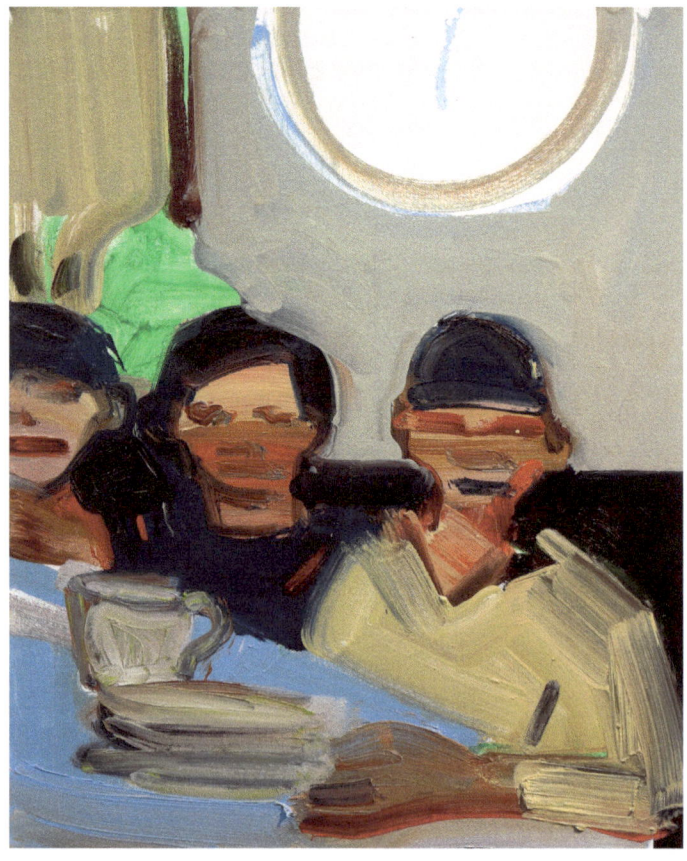

Katja Leibenath

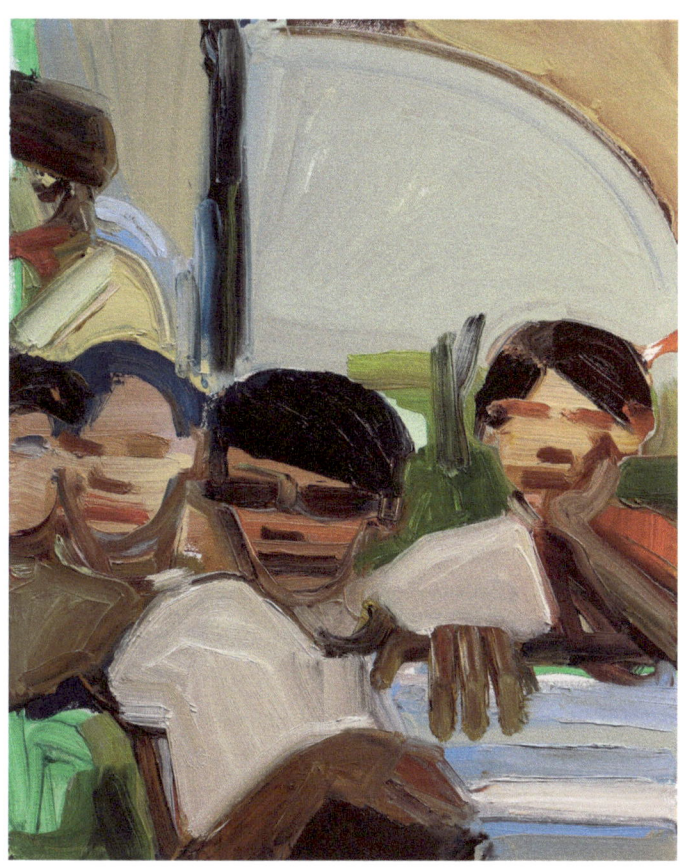

Seated Figures # 06

oil on canvas
20" x 16"
$1300

Seated Figure # 03

oil on canvas
20" x 16"
$1300

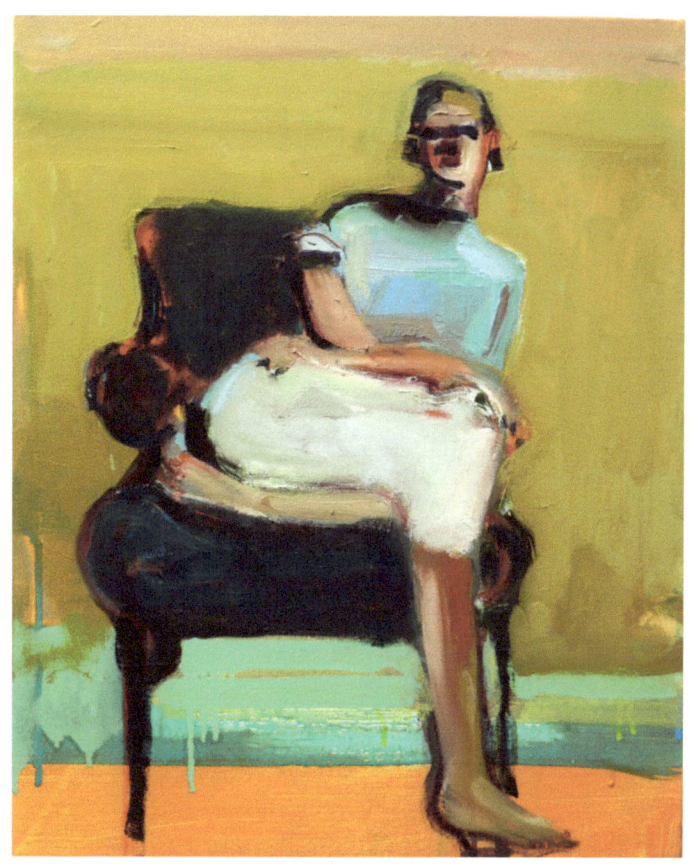

Katja Leibenath

Paul Morin

Nuclear Family

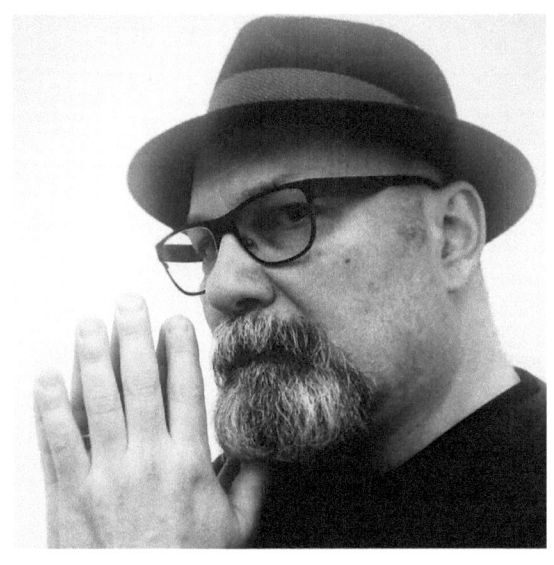

Hey boys and girls!

"One can have a great deal of fun playing hide and seek with a gamma ray source. Obviously, this game takes two or more people to play it. Estimates of what may happen in the future of science can often be prefaced with the apology that the 'Unexpected Usually Happens.' We shall tell you more information about radiation hazards later. Don't be alarmed by these things. They are just to inform you about the dangers that may exist. These hazards have been greatly exaggerated by the modern world. People often fear something they know very little about. The only way to make them forget these fears is to give them the facts.

"There has been so much misinformation about radioactivity that we pause here to reassure you and your parents that the radioactive sources supplied to you are not dangerous in any way.

"Science is not a magic black box from which one conjures up miracles at will. Rather we should say that science is a treasure chest which overflows with the basic ingredients for developing things of use to mankind. Science is such an unpredictable thing that one never knows just where the greatest benefits will arise. From our present outlook, it would seem that there will be no single atomic development which will constitute the greatest benefit to mankind. Rather the totality of the many aspects of atomic energy will be most significant. If the benefits of modern science and technology are used constructively, man will have within his reach the attainment of a truly more abundant life.

"Science is such an unpredictable thing that one never knows just where the greatest benefits will arise."

website:	http://www.studiomorin.com/
email:	paul@studiomorin.com

EDUCATION:
- Providence College
- Massachusetts College of Art

SELEECT EXHIBITIONS:

2019	*Twenty /Twenty,* ArtHaus Gallery, San Francisco CA
	Windows for Harvey, Stag and Manor, San Francisco CA
	Summertime, ArtHaus Gallery, San Francisco CA
	The Final Show, Wonderland SF, San Francisco CA
2018	*SHINE,* ArtHaus Gallery, San Francisco CA
	48 Pillars, Arc Gallery, San Francisco CA
	Fast Forward, ArtHaus Gallery, San Francisco CA
2017	*20th Anniversary Show,* ArtHaus Gallery, San Francisco CA
	BRUSHSTROKES-2017, San Luis Obispo Museum of Art, San Luis Obispo CA
	Summer Of Love, ArtHaus Gallery, San Francisco CA
	Delicous, STUDIO Gallery, San Francisco CA
	Project eARTh USA, Misho Gallery, San Francisco CA
	Salon 2017, Triton Museum Of Art, Santa Clara CA
2016	*Paul Morin Works,* Dolores Park Cafe, San Francisco CA
	Go Figure, ArtHaus Gallery, San Francisco CA
	Portraits and Digressions, ArtHaus Gallery, San Francisco CA
	Spectrum Gestalt 3, bG Gallery, Santa Monica CA
2015	*The Left Coast Annual Juried Show,* Sanchez Art Center, Pacifica CA
	SquaredAlumni, Arc Gallery, San Francisco, CA
	Cartes de Visite, Modern Relics Gallery, San Francisco CA
2014	Modern Past Gallery, San Francisco CA
	Found Portraits, Click Click Bang!! Salon and Gallery, Santa Cruz CA
2013	*Foursquared,* Arc Gallery, San Francisco CA
	Imaginarium Arc Gallery, San Francisco CA
	Cartes de Visite, Modern Relics Gallery, San Francisco CA
2012	*Emerging Artists 2012,* Driftwood Salon, San Francisco CA
	Red, O'Hanlon Art Center, Mill Valley CA
	Envisioned Enchanted, Wonderland SF, San Francisco CA
	Annual Juried Show, The Falkirk Cultural Center, San Rafael CA
	Primal Masquerade, Aspect1000 Gallery, San Francisco CA
	Modern Portraits, ArtZone461 Gallery, San Francisco CA
	Anniversary Show, ArtZone461 Gallery, San Francisco CA
	Notorious, Modern Eden Gallery, San Francisco CA
	Vintage Portraits, Classic Cars West, Oakland CA
2011	*Found Portraits,* Blush Wine Bar, San Francisco CA
	Illuminations, Nova, San Francisco CA
2009	Gallery 560, San Francisco CA
2008	Haven Home Furnishings, Carmel CA

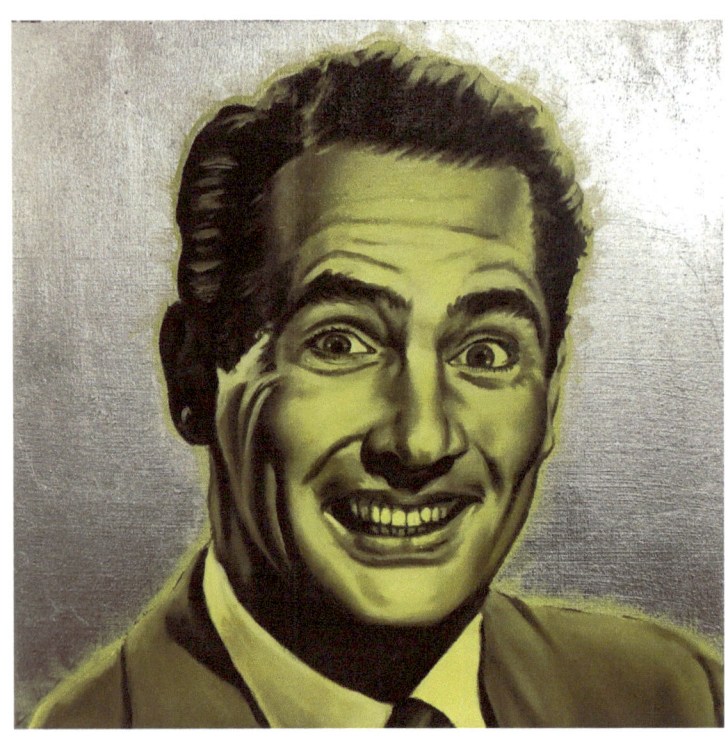

Father
oil and metal leaf on canvas
16" x 16"
$950

Mother
oil and metal leaf on canvas
16" x 16"
$950

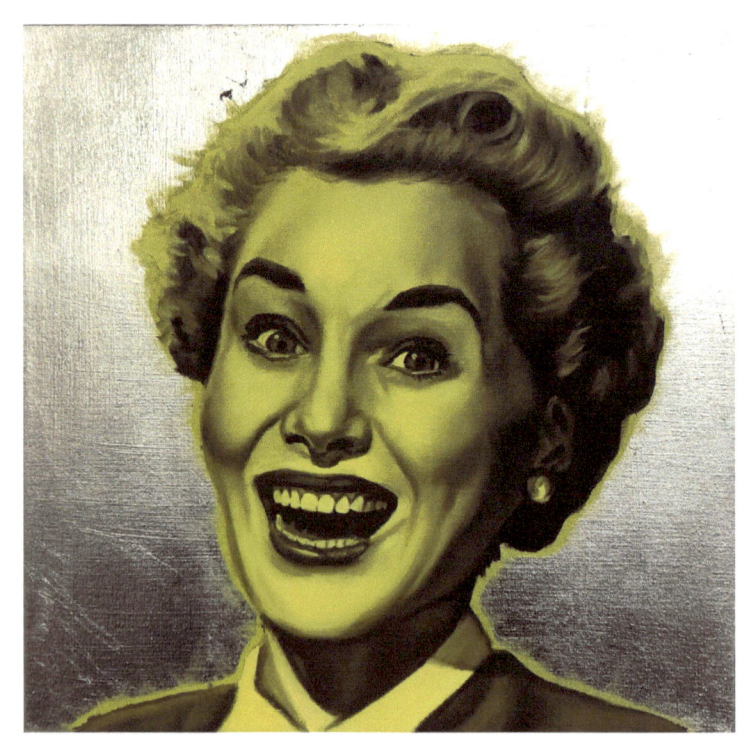

Paul Morin

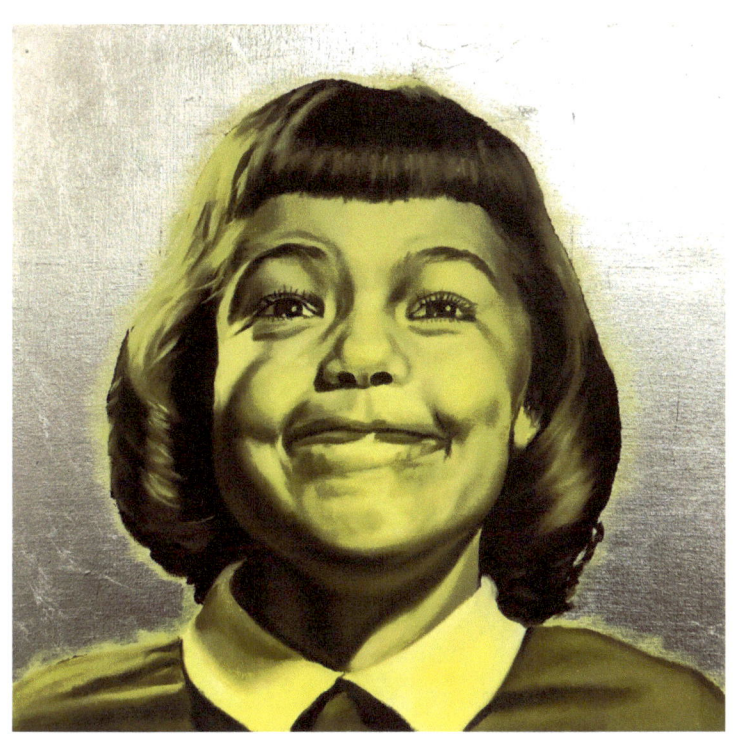

Sister
oil and metal leaf on canvas
16" x 16"
$950

Brother
oil and metal leaf on canvas
16" x 16"
$950

(set of four: $3000)

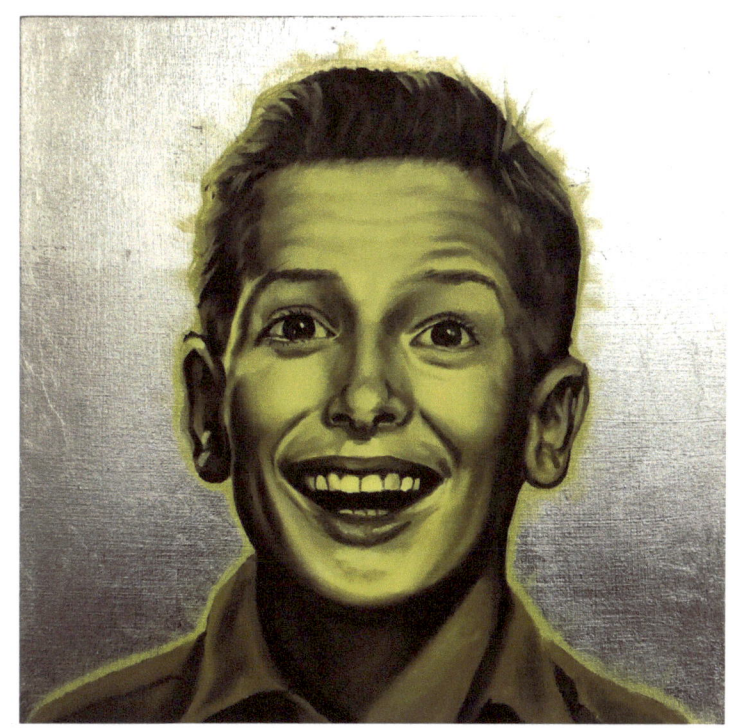

Paul Morin

Linda Raynsford

Talking Heads

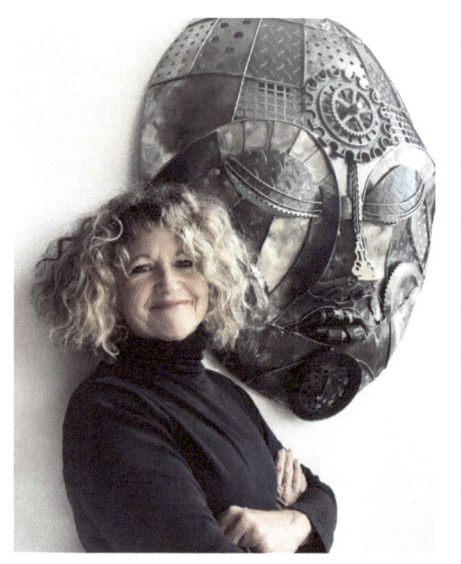

Like cooled lava, coursing through my veins and pouring out of me,—my metal sculpture is a reflection of personal reinvention through my own visual language. A language developed through years of curiosity and exploration to redefine what once was. From the time I was a little girl creating neighborhood productions using reimagined junk as costumes and props lying around in my dad's garage or my mom's antique costume collection, to my days in the fashion industry helping to create the illusion of beauty by reconceptualizing style. My fascination with unlimited usage for what people deem "junk" fueled my creative inspiration.

These pieces represent both my inner and outer narrative. My own metallic pentimenti. Showing more prominently the new creation but reinvention can never truly cover what once was entirely. You can always see glimpses of the former, which makes the latter all the more interesting.

website: http://lindaraynsford.com/
email: raynsford@mac.com

EDUCATION

BFA   California College of Arts and Crafts, Oakland CA

SELECTED EXHIBITIONS

2019	FM Gallery, Oakland	
2018	Chinatown Alley Gallery, Sacramento CA	
2017	Chinatown Alley Gallery, Sacramento CA	
2016	Skinner Howard, Sacramento CA	
	Skinner Howard, Sacramento CA	
2015	Campfire Gallery, San Francisco CA	
	Skinner Howard, Sacramento CA	
2014	Campfire Gallery, San Francisco CA	
2013	Skinner Howard, Sacramento CA	
2012	Nordstrom, Walnut Creek CA	
2009	Pamela Skinner Gallery, Sacramento CA	
2008	ArtZone Gallery, San Francisco CA	
	Pamela Skinner Gallery, Sacramento CA	
2007	Savage Art Gallery, Carmel CA	
2006	Pamela Skinner Gallery, Sacramento CA	
2005	Design Shop, Carmel CA	
	Wilkes Bashford, San Francisco CA	
2004	1212 Gallery, Burlingame CA	
2004	Excentrique, Sacramento CA	
2003	Excentrique, Sacramento CA	
2003	Sanchez Art Center, Pacifica CA	
2002	Excentrique, Sacramento CA	
2002	Space 743, San Francisco CA	
2001	ArtSmart, Linda Zweig/Fine Art, San Francisco CA	
2001	*New Work*, Excentrique, Sacramento CA	

SELECTED PUBLIC AND CORPORATE ART COMMISSIONS

Millbrae Bart Station & Gateway Project, Millbrae CA   NOMA Community, Richmond CA
Palomar Medical Center, Escondido CA   Stanford Medical Center, Palo Alto CA
One South Market Condominiums, San Jose CA   Camp Pendleton Naval Hospital, Oceanside CA
Saint John's Health Center, Santa Monica CA (w/ Reddy Lieb)   Children's Hospital, Los Angeles CA
John Muir Medical Center, Concord CA (w/ Reddy Lieb)   John Muir Medical Center, Walnut Creek CA

Kaiser Permanente, Earth's Breath, Dome Wall Monumentation, Irvine CA (w/ Reddy Lieb)
Glen Park Library, Six Degrees, Entry Wall Monumentation, San Francisco CA (w/ Reddy Lieb)

BIBLIOGRAPHY

2018	Sacramento Magazine
2008	Art Ltd Magazine, David Roth, January Issue
2002	Art Where You Least Expect It Robin Tunniclif, USA Weekend, Issue Aug.30-Sept. 1
2000	Show Boasts Gems Victoria Dalkey, Art Critic, Sacramento Bee
1999	Art Works in Sacramento Victoria Dalkey, Art Critic, Sacramento Bee
1999	At a Glance Victoria Dalkey, Art Critic, Sacramento Bee
1998	The Good the Bad & the Ugly Victoria Dalkey, Art Critic, Sacramento Bee

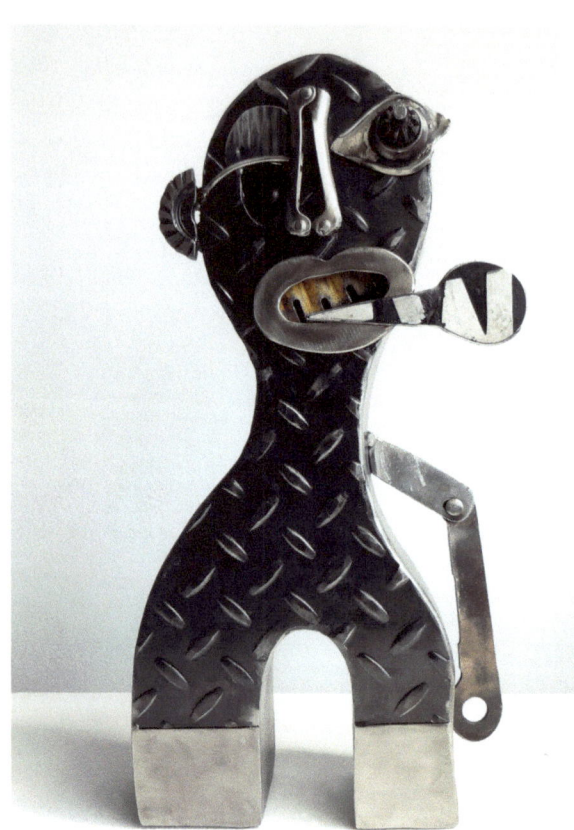

Bedtime Story
found steel and stainless with graphite
15.25" x 8" x 3.25"
$1600

Funny Bunny
found steel and stainless with graphite
12.5" x 10" x 7"
$1200

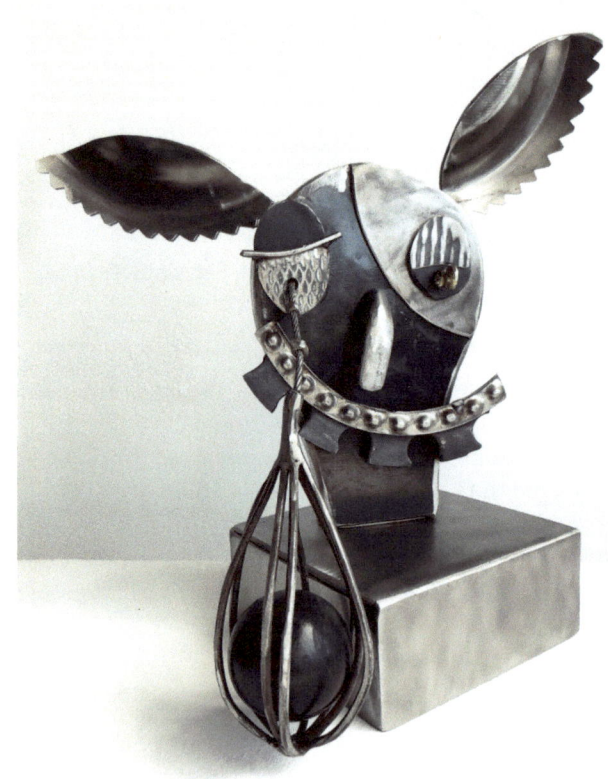

Linda Raynsford

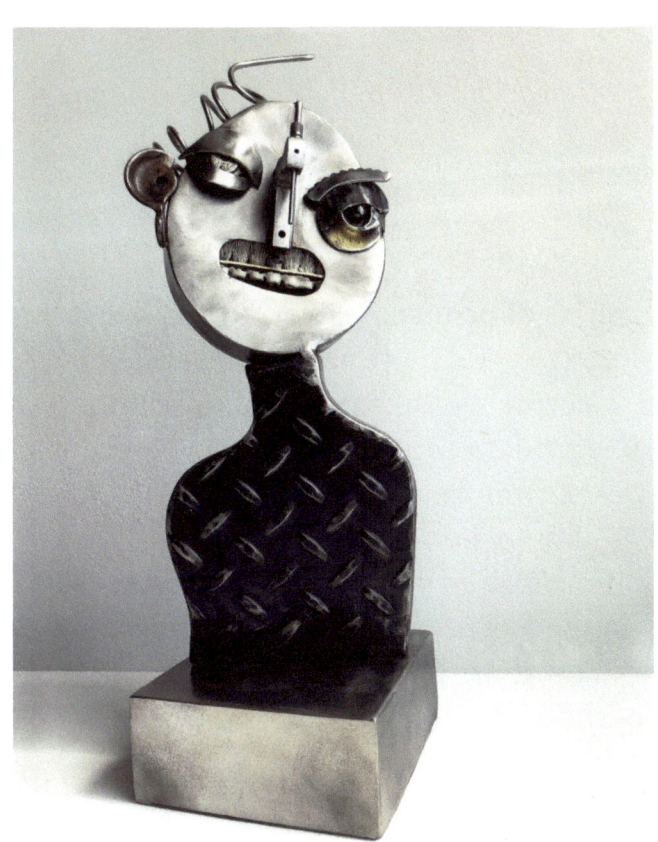

Strike A Pose
found steel and stainless with graphite
16" x 5.5" x 5"
$1900

Tight Rope
found steel and stainless with graphite
23" x 8" x 9.5"
$950

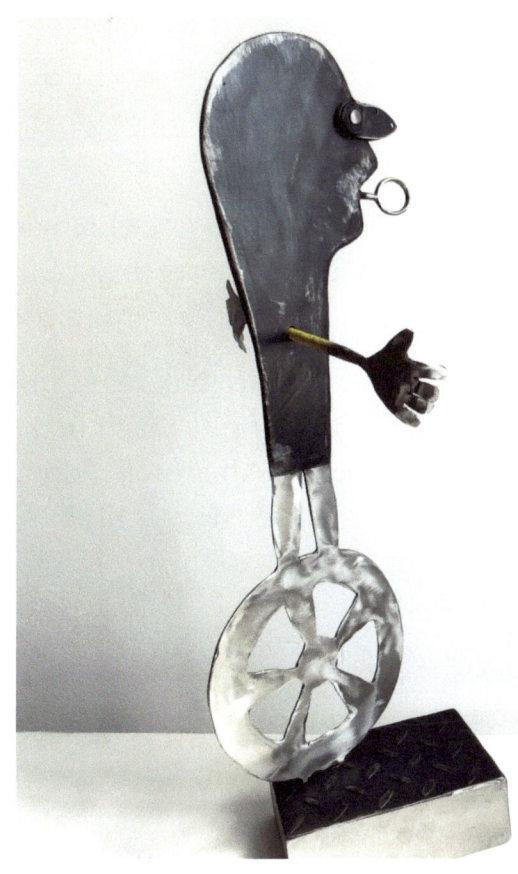

Linda Raynsford

Eric Rewitzer

Amador Flow

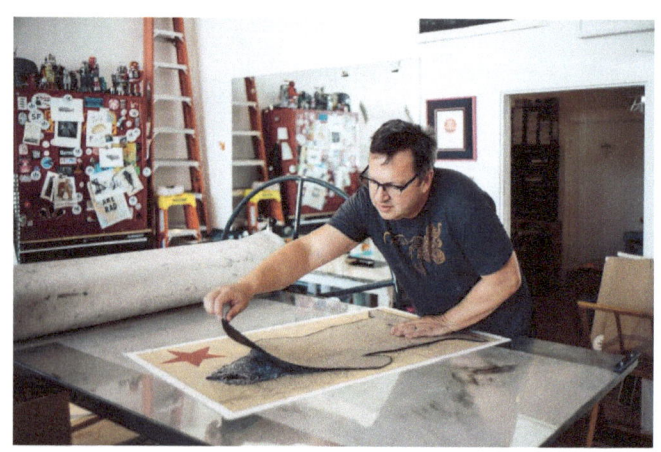

For this series of prints, I wanted to challenge myself creatively. Earlier this year, I traveled to Lincoln, Nebraska to take a workshop in the studio of legendary printmaker Karen Kunc, who taught me her unique technique of two block, double reduction woodcuts. Also this year, my wife and I purchased some property in Amador County in the Sierra Foothills, and I have been wanting to do some work inspired by the natural beauty of the area.

The result is this series, called Amador Flow, which is inspired by the Cosumnes River, which defines the northern edge of our new property. Water has beautifully carved away the granite rocks into organic, sensual shapes over the millennia. The palette is driven by water, sky, gold and the joy of being in nature.

For this show, I committed to make four unique prints, all with the two block double reduction technique that Karen taught me. Each print is 7 colors. I print from light to dark, alternating "water" and "stone" plates. After each color is printed, I remove more of the plate, and then ink it again with a darker color. There is little room for error, and each step needs to be carefully planned before committing to the press. At the end of the process, since so much of the plate has been removed, there is no way to reproduce the print; what you have printed during the process is what you get.

There are only five prints of each of these four images. I hope you enjoy this new direction in my work.

website: http://3fishstudios.com/
email: eric@3fishstudios.com

EDUCATION:

1986-87   Cleveland Institute of Art, Cleveland OH
1984-85   Michigan State University, East Lansing MI

SELECTED EXHIBITIONS, EVENTS & FAIRS:

2019   *This Must Be the Place*, 111 Minna Gallery, San Francisco CA (solo)
       48 Pillars, Arc Gallery, San Francisco CA
       StARTup Art Fair, Los Angeles CA
2018   StARTup Art Fair, Los Angeles CA
       Bond, Marin Community Foundation, Novato C   (solo)
       Sincerity and Sky, Secession Art, San Francisco CA
       Bear in Mind, the Story of the California Grizzly, History Museum of Sonoma County, Santa Rosa CA
       Invitational, Graton Gallery, Graton CA
       Big Ink, 3 Fish Studios, San Francisco CA
2017   *Land's End*, Rare Device, San Francisco CA Sausalito Art Festival, Sausalito CA
       Art for AIDS Live Auction, San Francisco CA
       ArtSpan Live Auction, San Francisco CA
       Roadworks, SF Center for the Book, San Francisco CA
2016   *Differing Feathers*, Great Highway Gallery, San Francisco CA
       City of Lights, L'Oeil Overt Gallery, Paris, France
       Hotel Biron, San Francisco CA   (solo)
       Sausalito Art Festival, Sausalito CA - 2nd Place, printmaking
       Madrone Art Bar, San Francisco CA   (solo)
       Art for AIDS Live Auction, San Francisco CA
       Roadworks, SF Center for the Book, San Francisco CA
       StARTup Art Fair, San Francisco CA
2015   *Roll The Presses*, Arc Gallery, San Francisco CA
2014   *SquaredAlumni*, Arc Gallery, San Francisco CA
       L'Oil Overt, Paris France
       Sausalito Art Festival, Sausalito CA
       invitationas, Graton Gallery, Graton CA
       Roadworks, SF Center for the Book, San Francisco CA
       Art for AIDS, San Francisco CA
       Hotel Biron, San Francisco CA   (solo)
2013   *Impulse*, Arc Gallery, San Francisco CA
       Roadworks, SF Center for the Book, San Francisco CA
       Hotel Biron, San Francisco CA   (solo)

COMMUNITY OUTREACH:

2012-18   ArtSpan, Board Member

PROFILE:

Full-time artist focusing on relief printmaking. Teacher, entrepreneur, and advocate for the arts in San Francisco
Owner: 3 Fish Studios, 4541 Irving St., San Francisco CA

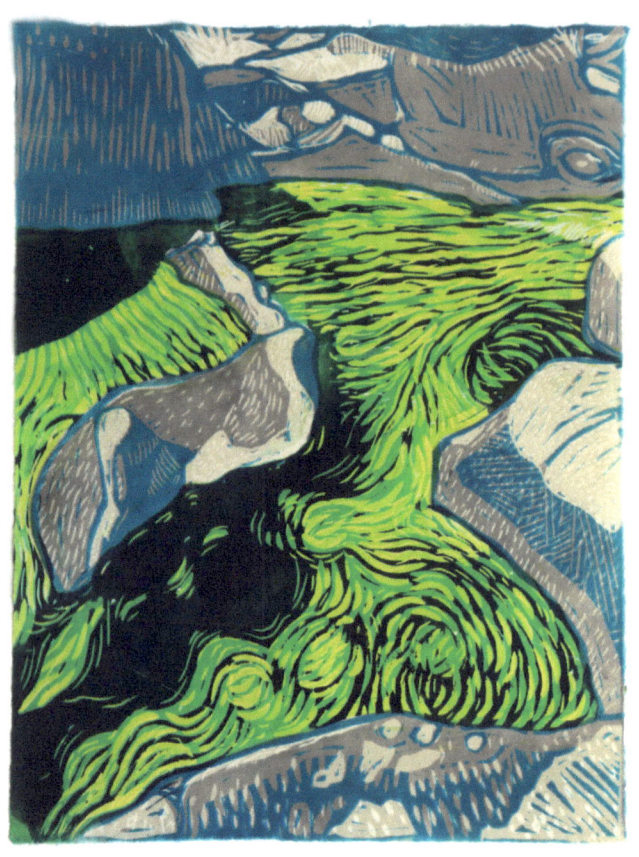

Amador Flow # 1
7-color woodcut on Nishinouchi paper
16" x 12" (framed 20" x 16")
$700 framed $2500 set of four framed
$350 unframed $1200 set of 4 unframed
edition 1 of 5

Amador Flow # 3
7-color woodcut on Nishinouchi paper
16" x 12" (framed 20" x 16")
$700 framed $2500 set of four framed
$350 unframed $1200 set of 4 unframed
edition 1 of 5

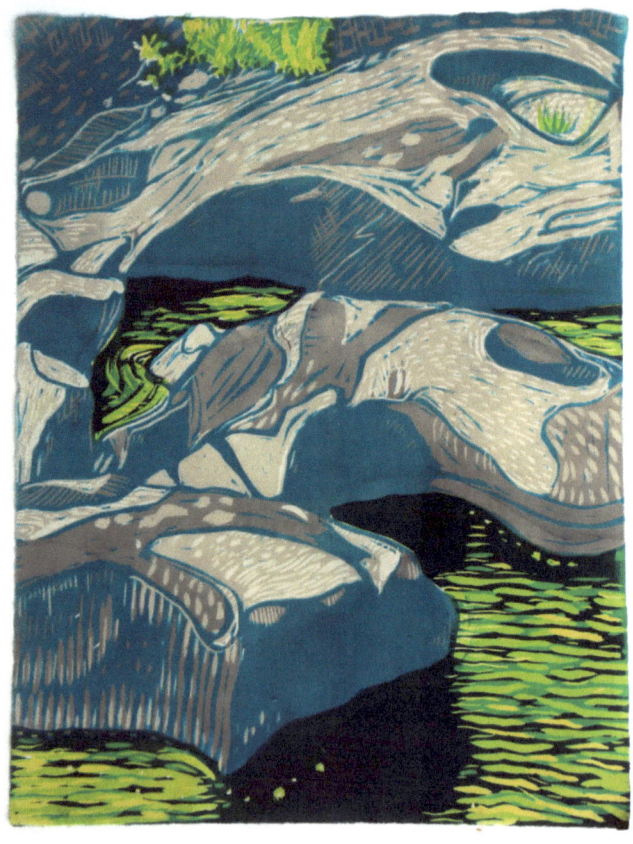

Eric Rewitzer

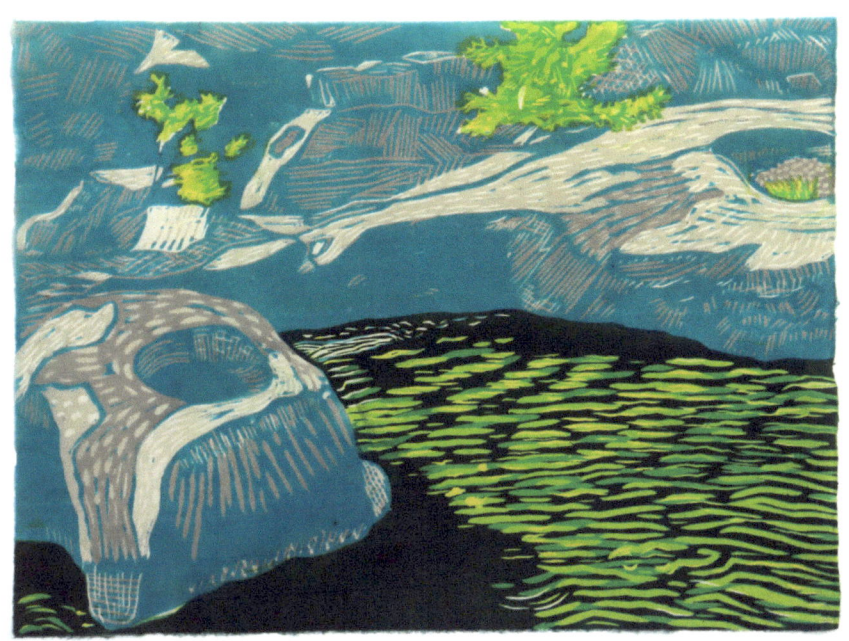

Amador Flow # 2

7-color woodcut on Nishinouchi paper
12" x 15" (framed 16" x 20")
$700 framed $2500 set of four framed
$350 unframed $1200 set of 4 unframed
edition 1 of 5

Amador Flow # 4

7-color woodcut on Nishinouchi paper
12" x 15" (framed 16" x 20")
$700 framed $2500 set of four framed
$350 unframed $1200 set of 4 unframed
edition 1 of 5

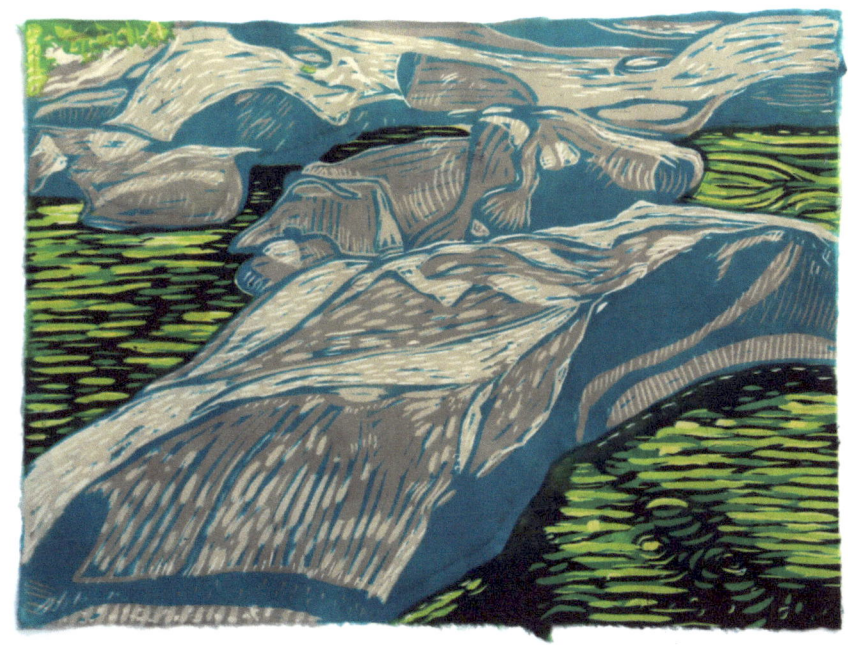

Eric Rewitzer

Rebecca Szeto

Fables & Fairy Tales

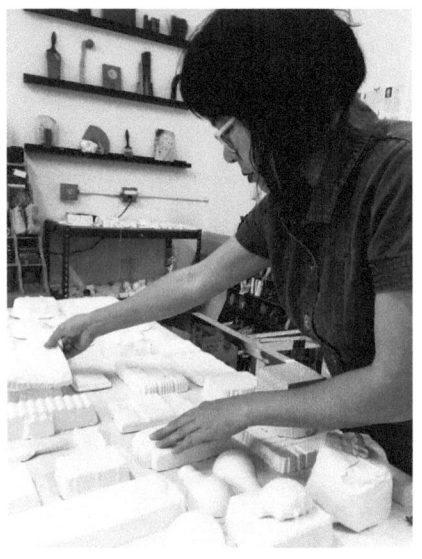

As someone who enjoys the small details of the everyday, much of my work is about making invisible moments visible. I am interested in the poetic intersection of the material and the immaterial -- a transformative, and often humorous synthesis of confounded expectations. The work focuses on objects, actions and situations that are normally overlooked or marginalized. Play and chance are integral parts of my process; in painting, I work from an intuitive place, exploring qualities and meaning below the surface of images. The results are oftentimes unpredictable, quietly playful, and contemplative.

website: http://rebeccaszeto.com/
email: rebecca@rebeccaszeto.com

EDUCATION

- 1992   B.A. in Studio Arts, University of California at Berkeley, Berkeley CA
- 1991   Language and Arts Program, Lorenzo de Medici, Florence, Italy

RECENT GROUP EXHIBITIONS

- 2017   *Fundraiser for Busajo Ethiopia*, La Loggia, Florence, Italy
  Fundraiser for Drawbridge for Kids, Twitter Headquarters, San Francisco CA
- 2016   *Emoticoncert*, Berl's Brooklyn Poetry Shop, Mew York City NY
  Art for Everybody, Chemeketa Community College, Sale OR
  Bizarre Bazaar, Root Division, San Francisco CA
- 2015   *Squared Alumni*, Arc Gallery, San Francisco CA
  Adaptations, Rovzar Gallery, Seattle WA
  Flirtations (Back Room), Jack Fischer Gallery, San Francisc, CA
  Left Coast Annual, Sanchez Art Center, Pacifica CA (curated by Cathy Kimball, ICA)
  Structure & Perspective, Snap! Space, Orland, Fl
- 2014   *Benefit Art Auction*, Artspan, San Francisco CA
  Paintbrush Portraits, Cisco Brothers, Los Angeles CA
- 2013   *One and Only*, Kohler Art Center, Sheboygan WI
  Fresh Art, Marin Society of Artists, Ross CA (curated by Rene de Guzman, Oakland Museum),
  Fictions, a.Muse Gallery, San Francisco CA
- 2011   *FourSquared*, Arc Gallery, San Francisco CA
  The Birds and the Bees, LinkSoul, Oceanside, CA
  Paintbrush Portraits, 505 Montgomery, San Francisco CA
- 2010   *Extreme Materials II*, Rochester Art Museum, Rochester NY (curated by Marie Via)
  Luminaries, Bryant Street Gallery, Palo Alto CA (2-person show)
- 2008   *Shifted Focus: APAture 10th Anniversary Retrospective*, Kearny Street Workshop, San Francisco CA
  Mapping Reason, Viva, Sebastopol CA
  Is This a Fiber Show, Bucheon Gallery, San Francisco CA
- 2007   *Art Basil Miami*, Bucheon Gallery, Miami FL

AWARDS & RESIDENCIES

- 2014   The Spiritual in Art Practice 3, Poppiano, Italy (Residencey)
- 2010   The Spiritual in Art Practice 2, Montagnana, Italy (Residencey)
- 2007   Domestic Departures, Cal State Fullerton, Santa Ana, CA (Residencey)
- 2005   Honorarium, APAture Featured Artist, Kearny Street Workshop, San Francisco CA
- 2004   CanSerrat, El Bruc, Spain (Residency, Full Stipend Recipient)
- 2004   Jo'burg & Limpopo, South Africa (Residency (Mar), with William Kentridge and Venda artists)
- 2003   Anderson Ranch Art Center, Snowmass CO (Residency Full Stipend Recipient (Jan-Mar))
- 2003   Pamela Joseph Fellowship for Minority Artists
- 2002   Banff Centre + Merit Scholarship, Banff, Canada (Residency)
- 2001   *Selections*, ArtSpan, San Francisco CA
- 1999   Michaelis Art Institute, Cape Town, South Africa (Residency)

COLLECTIONS & COMMISSIONS

Harper College, Palatine, IL • Merrill Lynch, SF, CA • Coi Restaurant, SF, CA • Fremantle Foundation, Fiesole, Italy
Privately held in Canada, Denmark, England, France, Italy, USA

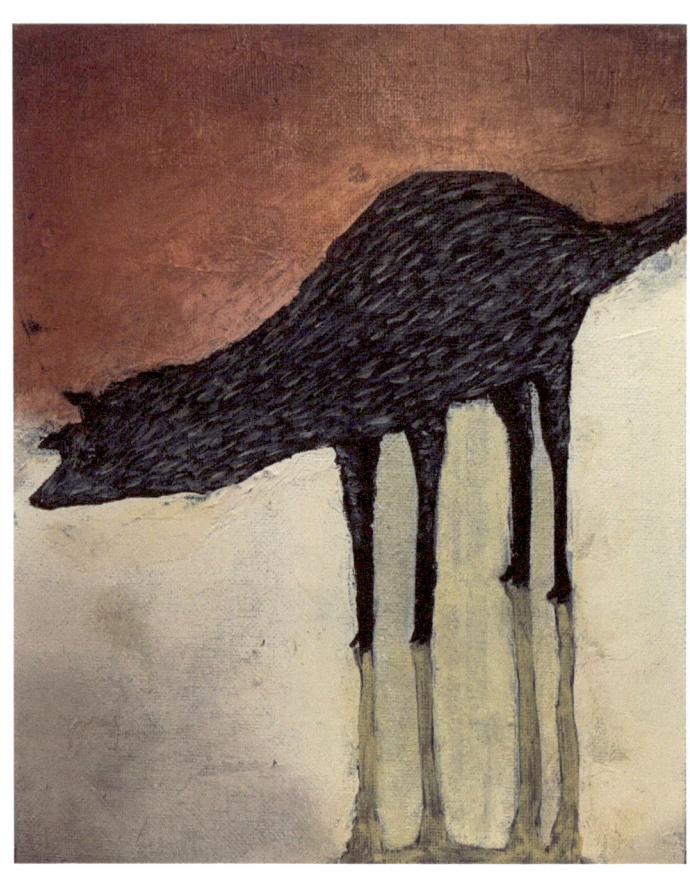

Mythic Creature

oil on canvas
10" x 8" x 3.25"
$750

Pony Up

oil on canvas
10" x 8" x 3.25"
$750

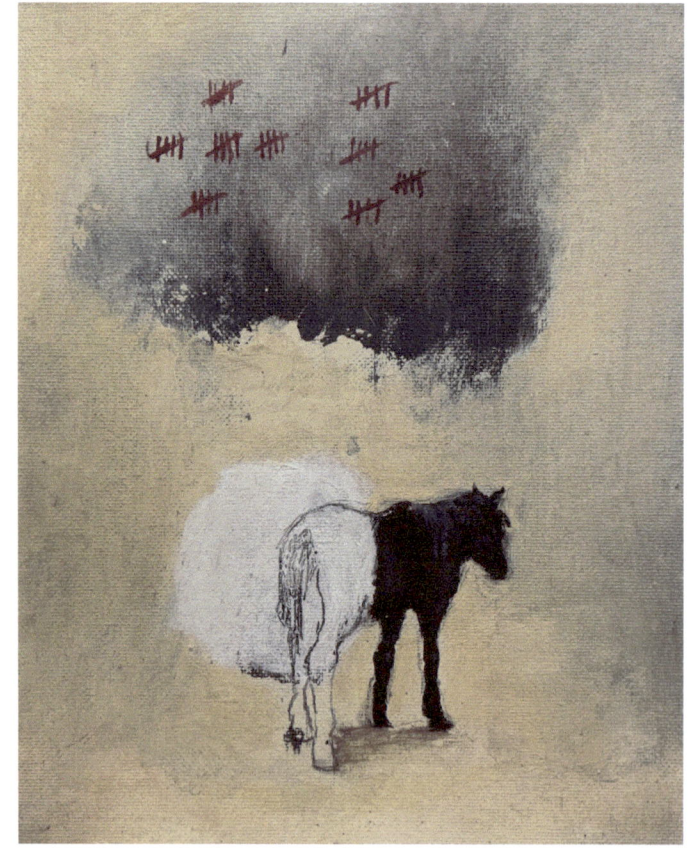

Rebecca Szeto

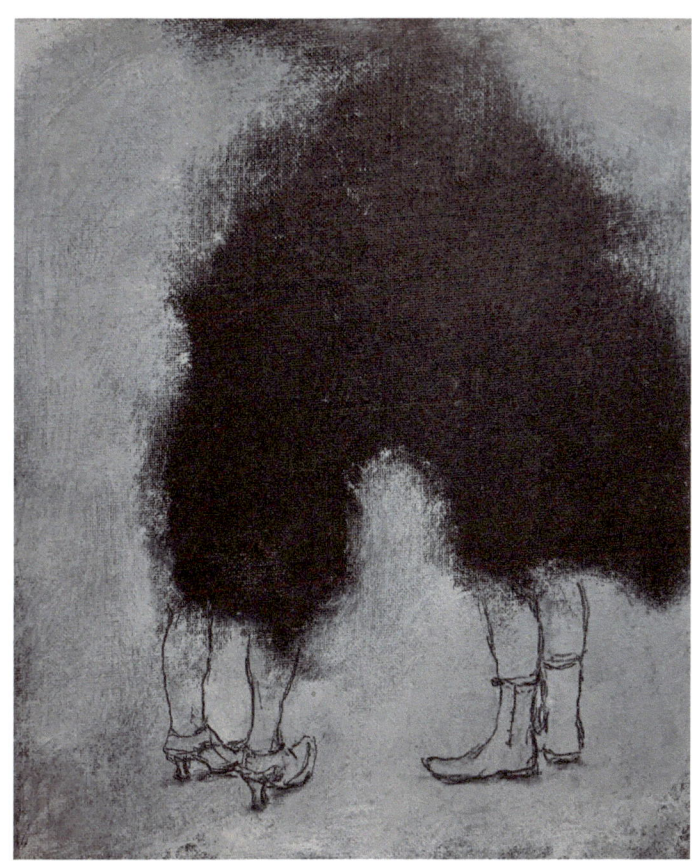

The Secret
oil on canvas
10" x 8" x 3.25"
$750

Wonder (Lucky Clover)
oil on canvas
10" x 8" x 3.25"
$750

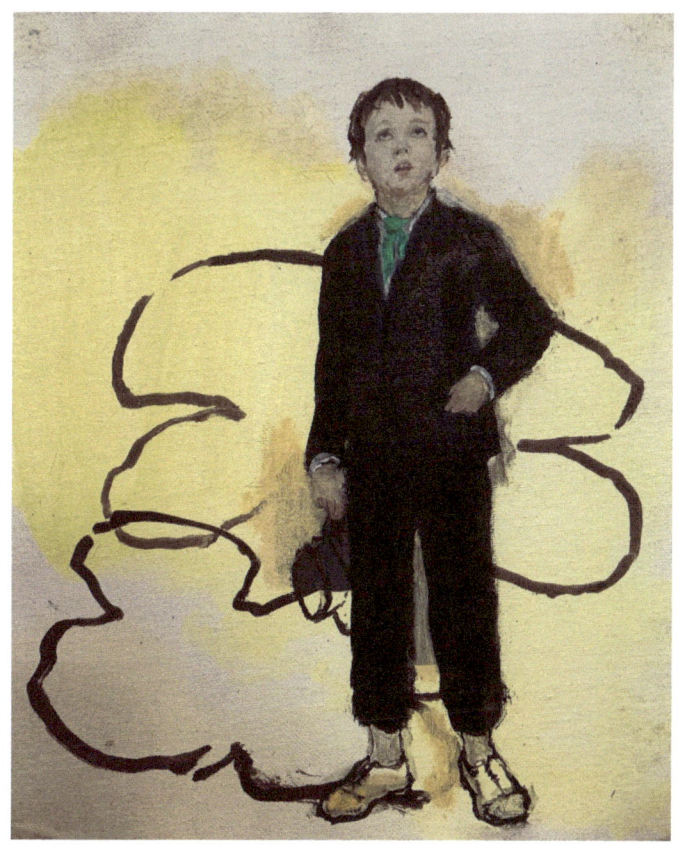

Rebecca Szeto

Melissa Wagner

The Arthropods

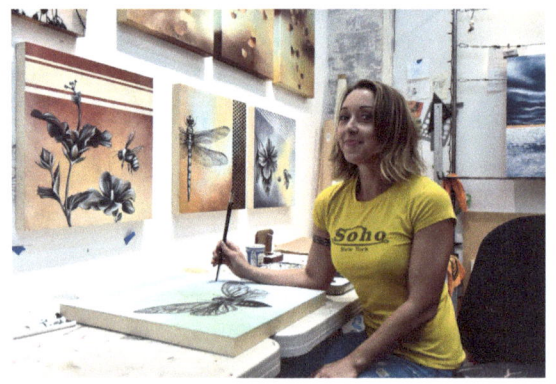

With a background in Scientific Illustration, Melissa Wagner's work uses a variety of methods and media to engage the natural world. Melissa playfully composes her vision of a world that harnesses natural subjects to construct new models of where art, earth, science and wonder intersect.

This new series brings to the forefront the importance of insects in our ecosystem. Roughly 600 species of insects are at risk of extinction worldwide. With insects making up 80 percent of all species on Earth, wiping out the insect population would have a huge effect on the web of life. For instance, if bees disappeared off the face of the earth, it is said that man would only have four years left to live.

website: http://www.wagnerpaintings.com/
email: melissa@wagnerpaintings.com

EDUCATION

1999   BFA   University of Michigan: major in Scientific Illustration; double major in Art and Biology

SELECTED EXHIBITIONS + INSTALLATIONS

2018   Four Barrel, San Francisco CA (solo)
2017   *FourSquared*, Arc Gallery, San Francisco, CA
        Commissioned Installation; Sarabeth's, Dubai, UAE
        Commissioned Installation; Sarabeth's, Nagoya, Japan
2016   *IMPULSE*; Arc Gallery, San Francisco. CA
2015   Commissioned Installation; Belga, San Francisco, CA
        Commissioned Installation; Delarosa Yerba Buena, San Francisco, CA
        Secession Gallery Grand Opening, San Francisco, CA
2014   *Flight*, solo show, Blackbird, San Francisco, CA
        Commissioned Installation; Delarosa Chestnut, San Francisco, CA
2013   Commissioned Installation; Barbacco Trattoria, San Francisco, CA
2012   Commissioned Installation; Hyatt Lone Eagle Grill, Incline Village NV
2011   Secession Gallery, Group show, San Francisco, CA
2010   Commissioned Installation; Twenty Five Lusk, San Francisco, CA
2008   *Re-connecting; 2nd Annual University of Michigan Alumni Show,* Ann Arbor, MI
2007   Solo Show; Benefitting Art for City Youth, San Francisco, CA
        10 years of Eco-Exploring;, University of Michigan Slusser Gallery, Ann Arbor, MI
        Multiple Choice; a juried multi-media exhibit, Sebastopol Center for the Arts, Sebastopol, CA
2005   *pARTicipate!*; Monkey Fresh Studios, San Francisco, CA
        Commissioned Installation for Chef Rick Moonen at RM Seafood, Mandalay Bay, Las Vegas, NV
2001   *Best of the Bay Show*, Culture Cache Gallery, San Francisco, CA
2000   *Spring Show*; Mad River Post, San Francisco, CA

RESIDENCIES + APPEARANCES

2014   Featured Speaker, National Association of Professional Women, San Francisco, CA
2007   "Celebrity Artist" Presenter at the Genetech Awards Presentation, San Francisco, CA
2003   Legion of Honor Artist in Residence Program, San Francisco, CA
        De Young Art Center Artist in Residence Program, San Francisco, CA
2002   Mural Project Director; Sanchez Elementary in San Francisco, CA
2001   East Palo Alto Charter School Mural Project Director, East Palo Alto, CA

PUBLICATIONS + AWARDS

2011   Architectural Record, Twenty Five Lusk Installation
2010   Contract Magazine, Barbacco Trattoria Installation
2009   People's Choice Award: University of Michigan Alumni Show, Ann Arbor, MI
        Artwork featured in "Top Chef Las Vegas" at RM Seafood at Mandalay Bay, Las Vegas, NV
2006   California Home & Design Magazine
2005   Hospitality Design Magazine, RM Seafood at Mandalay Bay Installation

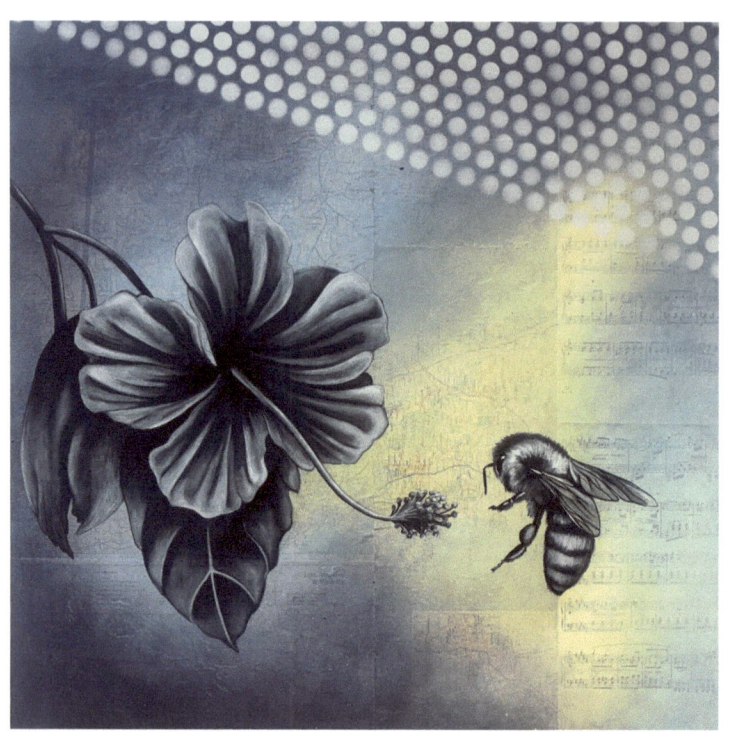

Anthophila+Hibiscus 1
mixed media
20" x 20"
$1200

Anthophila+Hibiscus 2
mixed media
20" x 20"
$1200

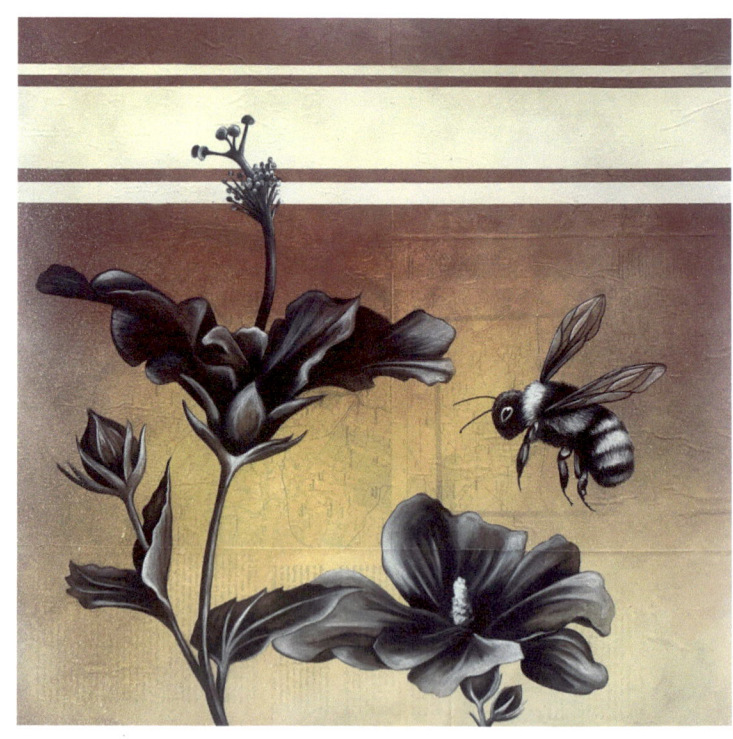

Melissa Wagner

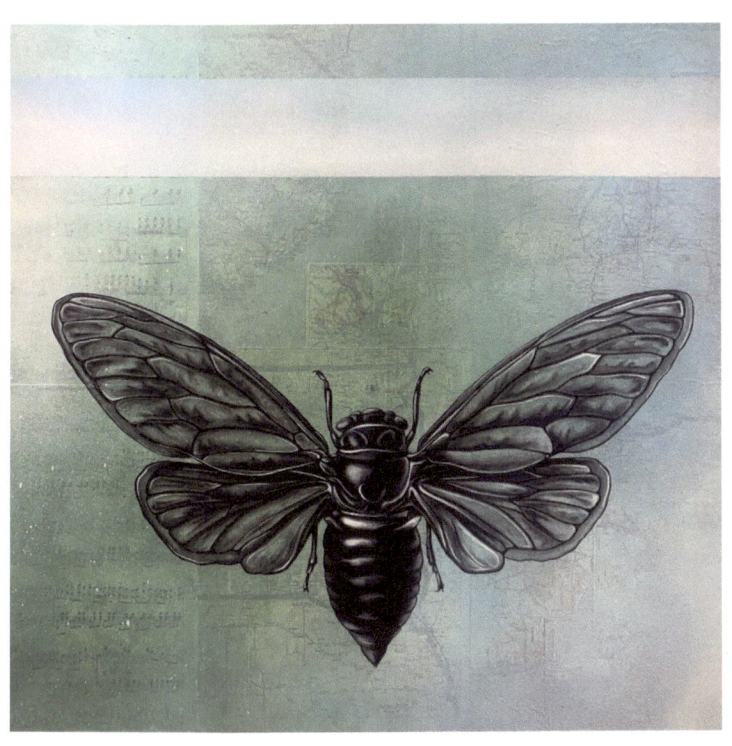

Aphidoidea
mixed media
20" x 20"
$1200

Anisoptera
mixed media
20" x 20"
$1200

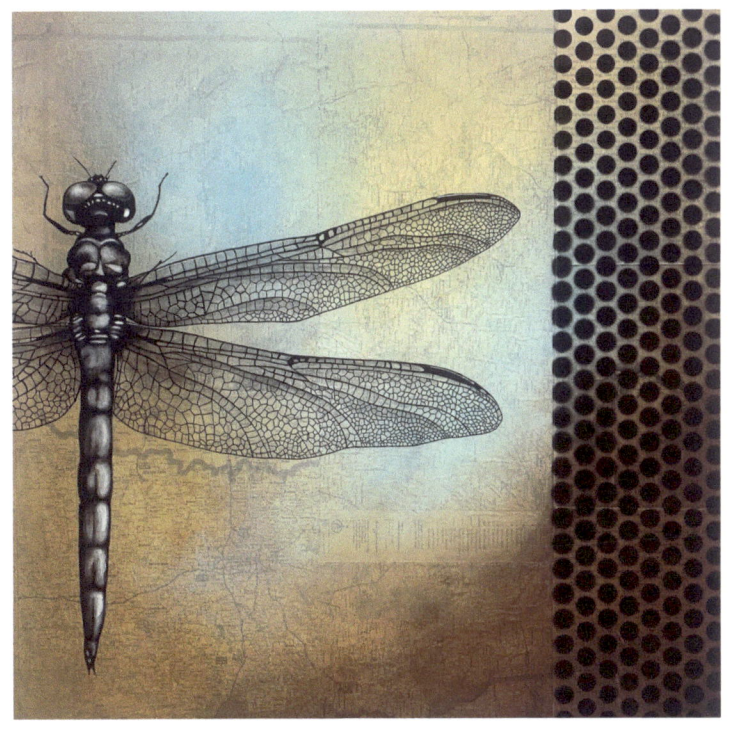

Melissa Wagner

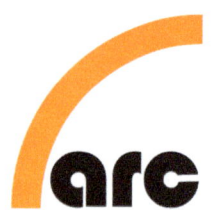

gallery
project gallery
studios
fine art consulting

1246 Folsom St.
San Francisco, CA

http://arc-sf.com
http://arcfinearts-sf.com
arcgallerysf@gmail.com
415-298-7969

www.ingramcontent.com/pod-product-compliance
Lightning Source LLC
Chambersburg PA
CBHW040451220526
45473CB00004B/1595